BECOMING AN EVOLUTIONARY WAYSHOWER

by
Zoran TODOROVIC
with
Ushma PATEL, Soleira GREEN, and Jane MACALLISTER DUKES

PUBLISHED BY
The New Millennium (TNM) Coaching
www.tnmcoaching.com

Zoran Todorovic, Ushma Patel, Solera Green and Jane McAllister Dukes
asserts the moral right to be identified and the authors of this work.

PHOTOGRAPHS BY
Vincent Ledvina (Unsplash), Miguel Bruna (Unsplash), Ian Stauffer (Unsplash),
Guillaume de Germain (Unsplash), Denys Nevozhai (Unsplash), Nghia Le (Unsplash)

© TNM (TNM Coaching)

All rights reserved. No part of this publication may be reproduced, stored, in a retrieval system or transmitted in any form or by any means, electronic, mechanical, photocopying, recording or otherwise, without the prior permission of the publishers.

CON
TENT

Introduction	12

COURSE ONE — THE LIVING MIND — 18

Chapter I: The Open Mind	21
Chapter II: Accessing Passion and Vision	29
Chapter III: Coaching Possibilities	37
Chapter IV: Coaching Clarity and Conscious Choice for Evolution	46
Chapter V: Coaching Balance and Flow	52
Chapter VI: Coaching Alignment Through Essence	59
Chapter VII: Coaching Creation	64
Chapter VIII: Coaching Abilities in the Living Mind	73
Chapter IX: Coaching Evolutionary Intelligence	80
Chapter X: Coaching Levels of Potential	86
Chapter XI: Coaching the Evolution of Self	93
Chapter XII: Coaching Evolutionary Living	98
The Living Mind Wrap-Up	104

COURSE TWO — THE LIVING SOUL — 108

Chapter I: A Road Map to Wholeness Through The Alchemical Heart, the Integrated Spirit, and the Holistic Soul	111
Chapter II: Evolving Soul in the Evolutionary Paradigm	122
Chapter III: Profound Potential - Coaching the Brilliance and Power of Innate Being	131
Chapter IV: Beyond Breakthrough... Reality Creation Extraordinaire	141
Chapter V: Sourcing and Coaching Vibrant, Creative Genius	150
Chapter VI: The Power Of Living Soul	158
The Living Soul Course Wrap-Up	168

COURSE THREE — EVOLUTION — 172

Chapter I: Visionary Stewardship	175
Chapter II: ALLchemy	183
Chapter III: Creational Life Power	190
Course Wrap-Up: Evolutionary Strategy	194

INTRODUCTION

Welcome to the Advanced Evolutionary Coaching Training programme!

If you're reading this, you are likely an experienced coach who wants to move beyond coaching everyday success to coaching the evolution of humanity and of global transformation. You are ready to become an Evolutionary Wayshower.

Coaches hold in our collective hands the power to evolve and create a different world, a world that recognizes that we are all interconnected as one—and at the same time, that we are here to become completely and fully all that we are as unique individuals. It is time to evolve our profession and create that world.

Through this Advanced Evolutionary Coaching Training Text and programme we will help you to re-connect profoundly to your own magnificence and from there, discover how to coach and facilitate the movement of the human experience through its path of evolution. This textbook will help you become more skilled as an evolutionary coach and be trained to become Evolutionary Wayshowers.

WHAT IS AN EVOLUTIONARY WAYSHOWER?

An Evolutionary Wayshower is a master planner, architect, designer, creator, builder, and implementer of our vast, co-creational future that touches everything everywhere. They not only dance in and impact awareness, but create and evolve it as well. They know that evolution is not a million-year process where we go merrily along for the ride. They know that every breath and every action we take has the potential to evolve Life everywhere on this Earth and beyond.

Evolutionary Wayshowers are not just working on projects, companies, education, politics, or for that matter any one single thing in this world. They are working on the whole of it: the future of human kind, of the Earth, of this evolving cosmos and beyond. They look not just to the impact we have on ourselves and our world. They look to the impact we have on everything everywhere.

Evolutionary Wayshower is a role that one takes on proudly, profoundly, passionately, and powerfully. It calls to those who are truly meant to dance within it, who are skilled beyond measure in seeing beyond where they presently reside. You may ask, can a human body be the centre point for this much wisdom, knowledge, and awareness? Absolutely! It's what we were always designed to be and do. Through this Advanced Evolutionary Coaching training course, we at TNM Coaching are delighted to show you how.

WHAT'S IN THIS BOOK

The Advanced Evolutionary Coaching training course and textbook are divided into three courses:

COURSE ONE —
The Living Mind
In this course you will learn how to move beyond mind- and head-based intelligence to begin to live ultra-connected as the living intelligence that surrounds us and fills us from within. We will explore how to dance with our clients, energetically and in Living Mind, with our knowing and sensing intact. You will learn to see, smell, and taste potential everywhere and to know how to alchemise it into being graciously and powerfully.
You will become a Potentialist.

COURSE TWO —
The Living Soul
In this course you will begin to move you coaching into the realms of evolving beingness. We will play with the move from essence to essentiALLity and the liberation of human beings from that which they were born as. We will create the possibility for us to live as creational beings in every moment, dipping into a new geniUS pool for all possibilities. We will begin to

coach the evolution of human beingness and to explore reality creation.
You will become an Alchemist and Creationalist.

COURSE THREE —
Evolution

In course 3, you will explore the whole wonderful field of evolution—the evolution of coaching, of leading, of being, of living, of loving, and of so much more. We will play with even more levels of ALLchemy for our profound and powerful mindful evolution.
You will become a vibrant, Life-sourcing Evolutionary Wayshower.

Learning Objectives
- To coach your mind so that you can discover the freedom and creation of an open mind.
- To completely re-engineer and evolve how we coach the mind.
- To coach mind to limitless beliefs and possibilities.
- To consciously coach life using possibilities and probabilities to create the life experiences clients want to create right now.
- To coach full empowerment through knowing that we create our own reality.
- To coach others be make clear, conscious choices, regardless of the scenario.
- To coach others to access the profound state of alignment and balance, being in a flowing dance with creation.
- To coach equilibrium through the alignment of flow.
- To coach others to discover that life is one big creative act.
- To coach others to move freely into living, evolutionary intelligence.
- To coach emotional intelligence and spiritual intelligence to evolutionary levels.
- To coach others to align themself and others with essence, passion and what wants to be.
- To coach the pure and profound energy of passion and vision for yourself and for others.
- To be able to access, coach, understand and experience all the levels of self
- To understand, coach to further create the evolution of soul in the evolutionary paradigm.
- To be able to coach and source genius in yourself and others on unprecedented levels.
- To be able to coach and source super-creativity, original thinking and visionary living in yourself and others.
- To coach others to co-create new levels of power.
- To coach others to see that we are all mega human beings with a contribution to make.
- To coach others to use their magical abilities.
- To coach people to the level of profound motivation by accessing pure passion, which creates the energy of movement to inspire purest action.
- To open the incredibly exciting door to limitless possibilities and to give you and those you coach access to living as them.
- To know how to activate creational Life power in those you coach

This is a leaderful time when the gems of each and every person's contributions can be gifted to global creations that move humanity and ALL forward. We invite you to join this magnificent community of Evolutionary Wayshowers, committed to breaking the boundaries of learning and sharing with one another our unique abilities that allow us to co-create a whole new world!

COURSE ONE

THE
LIVING
MIND

CHAPTER I
THE OPEN MIND

Intention Of This Chapter
- To discover the freedom and creativity of an open mind.
- To explore the possibilities an evolving mind can offer.

Profound Potential
- To completely re-engineer and evolve how the mind operates.
- To liberate the mind—to discover the real power of OPEN
- To "blow your mind" to limitless possibilities.

Key Elements

1 — From closed to open
A "how-to" manual for opening your mind.

2 — Plugging in
Exploring the mind as a computer and hooking it to the "consciousness" internet.

3 — Navigation
Finding your way into new intelligence, new abilities, and areas of consciousness

4 — Moving into knowing
Becoming the engine for the perspective, insights, wisdom that are needed and wanted in the moment.

5 — The mindful dance
The effortless, rhythmic dance

6 — The conscious mind
Engaging with limitless possibilities

Exploratory Discussion
1. Are you working with an open mind?
2. Can you recognize when others are working with an open mind?
3. Do you think intelligence is something that you're born with and is measurable by IQ? Or do you believe intelligence is something that we can connect to and is immeasurably available to all?
4. What does "never mind" mean to you? What does it feel like to go beyond mind?
5. Can we know anything and everything?
6. Are we part of a greater mind, a vaster intelligence?

ESSENTIAL CONTENT

1 — From closed to open

We have just entered a new millennium, a new era, and the distinct shift from the last millennium to this one is most exemplified in our relationship to mind. Throughout the last thousands of years, human beings have mostly lived in a closed energy system—closed minds, hearts, spirits and souls. It is the closed mind that has brought us to where we are today and it is the expanded mind that will lead the way into this new era to create an unprecedented future for us all.

Are you working with an open mind?
Are you open to new ideas?
Are you willing to consider that we are only just beginning to touch the edges of human possibility?
Do your beliefs limit or constrict you in any way?
Do you adventure with your mind, seeking new possibilities for things that you do?
Are you willing to entertain that the mind is NOT contained within the human head?

Exercises

To open your mind or that of someone you're coaching, try these simple exercises:

· **Energy check** – Where is your energy primarily located in your body right now? In your head or is it in some other part of you? If it's mostly in the area of your head, try shifting the energy to some other part of the body (heart, hands, chin, feet, etcetera) and see how it feels.

· **Passion** – Think of anything you're passionate about (chocolate, scuba diving, or saving the world) and notice how you feel when you do that. Passion opens the high heart (breastplate area), freeing the mind. As you think about the passion, feel where the energy moves from and to in your body.

· **Expansion** – Take a deep breath and relax your body and mind. Then allow yourself to expand, feeling the edges of you get bigger and bigger. Allow yourself to expand to the point that you're comfortable with. For some people that will be as big as the room you're in, for others as big as the Earth and beyond. Explore just how big you're willing to be and what you're willing to discover in this expanded state. Notice how different your mind feels and functions.

· **Exploring thoughts and beliefs** – If you're not able to expand in the way described, then ask yourself what thoughts or beliefs you have that are keeping you from ex panding. You can do this for your clients too to move them to an open mind.

It's not about changing their beliefs to something different; it's about exploring the beliefs they have to see if they energetically and experientially limit their lives. You can ask, "Is this true for you now?"

Often the mind can hold onto belief long past its expiry date, and freeing people of these old and no longer valid beliefs can open up the possibility for them to be, to create, and to live more powerfully present in the now.

· **Intention** – If all else fails, simply intend to have an open mind and see what happens. Intention has within it the power to fuel the universes.

2 — Plugging in

What is the energetic source point for new ideas and for creation? Is it the brain or is it from some other source? Ideas do end up in the mind, because that is the final resting point for our conscious awareness, but where do they originate from?

We believe that ideas and creativity originate from a variety of other places—the heart, the spirit, the soul, the air—none of which are located inside the head. If you want to discover super-creativity and ultra-thinking, then explore the knowledge and possibilities that are all around us and deep within us. Go beyond the mind and plug into the super-brain, the Living Mind that is our natural way of being.

Perhaps the mind is like a computer; what's in your brain is what's already there, like the programmes stored in a computer. When the computer is working on a standalone basis, it can only access the programmes that are contained within it. But when the computer is plugged into the internet (i.e., super-connected to the vast, limitless intelligence of the universe), a whole wealth of information, insights, perspectives and more are on offer! It becomes the Living Mind.

Exercises

How do you super-connect? There's not just one, two or three ways...there may be as many ways as there are people. Explore, create and discover the ways that work best for you.

· **Sense, don't think** – To plug in, simply expand your sensing into the air around you. What is that like? Ask a question and *allow* the answer to come to you. Do not use your brain to *think* an answer. Instead feel out around you from an open and expanded state and see what answers, ideas, and suggestions come to you. Super-connect with the air and the intelligence around and within you. This is literally being "out of your mind."

· **Visualize the possibilities in the air** – Another way to plug in is to visualise millions of little antennae coming from you and "plugging into" the spaces in the air around you. What if every one of those spaces in the air is a space of possibility, an access point to immense knowledge and wisdom, a white hole into vast intelligence? Play with it, try it out, see how it feels.

· **Connect with your whole being** – Consider that your body, emotions, feelings, and senses are your barometer. Perhaps we are always plugged in and connected but we are not necessarily conscious of it in our minds. Perhaps the body, emotions, feelings, and senses are the vast intelligence communicating with us. Consider that you're a hologram (or better yet, a "whole-ogram") and that every cell in your body is actually all the cells in all the universes. Notice if you become more alert as you do this. Does your curiosity rise? Do you feel differently about things? Are you super-connecting into something bigger than yourself? How does that feel?

3 — Navigation

Once you're operating with an open mind and plugged into the Living Mind and vast intelligence, the next step is to learn how to navigate within it. But don't try to figure it out with your mind. Allow yourself to free-flow, to simply plug in and connect. Feel the rhythm of the Living Mind space and allow yourself to move into it and with it. This is a pure energetic space, a space of conscious knowing, wisdom, innate sensing and more. Let its rhythm navigate this new territory for you.

Exercises

There are many ways to free flow into the pathways of the Living Mind:

· **Move into consciousness** – Consciousness is an experiential state and is not the same as conscious awareness. *Conscious awareness* is being aware of life around you. *Consciousness* is where potential is seeded and where intelligence is evolved—beyond time, space or form. Think of consciousness as the alchemist's playground.

Allow yourself to move beyond mind into the Living Mind, into consciousness, where navigation becomes automatic. You know where to go as you follow the pathways of your conscious intent. In consciousness, distance falls away and your friends and family are right there beside you regardless of where you or they are in the world. Try it: Tune in to one of your good friends now in consciousness. Simply connect into the Living Mind and then intend to connect with your friend. Visualise them right there in front of you. You'll discover they're actually energetically right there with you as you connect with them.

· **Access creation** – Creation is the womb of all potential, possibilities, and ideas before they're seeded and birthed. Creation is also a process of bringing things from conception into realisation. To access creation from the Living Mind, visualise sliding through your heart space into the air in front of you. We call this the ocean of soul or the sea of possibilities. Then allow yourself to dive deep beneath the sun-lit ocean into a vast cavern of sparkling jewels (the pure creation space), each jewel a potential or possibility just waiting to be conceived into living reality. Just be open and allow the movement to begin. Again, you don't have to force the navigation here. If the visualisation doesn't quite work for you, then just intend to access pure creation and see where that leads you.

· **Make a conscious choice for exploration** – Allow yourself to expand from your center, to be as energetically big as you can be. It's like allowing your conscious awareness to keep getting bigger and bigger, all the while staying right here in the now. See if you can get bigger than the Earth and even as big as the cosmoses. There is a point, if we keep on getting bigger and bigger, that we discover that we are everything, we are ALL.

This is actually a very simple state to achieve. Just keep expanding and suddenly you discover that whoosh you are there. This is the state of ALL-ness. In our closed energy system state, achieving ALL-ness used to take years of concentrated meditation and focus, but today in our open energy system, it only takes a few seconds and you're there.

How does ALL-ness feel? Peaceful, serene, lovely, connected? These are words that people often use to describe this state. If your experience is different, that's great! After all this is ALL-ness and that means that everything is contained within it.

Often on the journey into ALL-ness, people stop at the peaceful point. But we're going to ask you to step beyond that by making a conscious choice for exploration. Make a conscious decision about where to go and what to explore and see what happens. Become the force for change in your conscious reality.

· **Surrender and trust** – There is adventure in surrendering and trusting. There is a magnetic force that takes us where we need to go. Our minds do not need to navigate and control, only to surrender to this magnetic force, to be guided to new and amazing discoveries. We can consciously choose where to navigate (by applying our own conscious intention) or we can surrender to the possibilities and allow ourselves to free flow into mega-discovery.

4 — Moving into knowing

Close your eyes and consciously connect to *the knowing inside of you*. Where is it located? Hint: It's not in your mind. Ask questions and allow the knowing to take you into exploration. Your mind expands into the Living Mind and you become alert, open, free—without filters. Trust what comes to you in this inner knowing state. Inner knowing is richer, deeper and tends to be more personally oriented. It's that which you have always known.

Think of inner knowing like your personal intra-net. Alternatively, *the knowing outside of you* is like a cosmic internet. It is the knowing in the air around you, containing all that has been and will be. All this information is there externally for you to plug in to, browse through and select from. In this space, you become the search engine for the perspective, insights, wisdom and knowing of what is needed and wanted in the moment.

Exercises

· **Connecting to inner / outer knowing** – Can you connect with both your inner and outer knowing at the same time. Does it feel different from doing each one individually? How?

Whatever comes to you, use it unfiltered and unedited. Your body will tell you if you've got the answer or perspective you're looking for. There's a settled, complete feeling when you get it and a less settled and less complete feeling when you haven't quite found that perfect perspective yet. If you haven't quite found that perfect perspective, then question this inter- and intra-net of intelligence further until you have what it is you seek. Once you get it, there's generally an a-ha feeling and an empowering perspective slips into place.

· **Trust and practice** – Knowing is a natural skill for us. So we recommend trust and practice with your knowing. Play with it. Use life's situations and your clients' explorations to discover just how much the Living Mind can gift you.

5 — The mindful dance

There is a symphony in Living Mind. Different chords weave together, like music playing, and an ecstatic version of reality is possible when you allow the music, the rhythm to take you. Life becomes a dance among people, situations, moments, and energy. When you feel the rhythm of this Mindful Dance, you become a part of the vast orchestra of collective creative intelligence. Now your mind is really open and full.

Exercise

If you try to make this happen with your brain-mind, it can be a lot of work. Instead, open up and simply allow it to happen.

· **From awareness to effortless awareness** – Begin to move to the rhythm of the music and the dance. Surrender control and effortlessly *become* the music and the dance.

> Call upon the sensations of listening to your very favorite music, swaying and moving to the rhythm. It's exactly the same in expanded, conscious intelligence. Love the experience and allow yourself to let loose with the dance.
>
> When you're coaching someone, first allow yourself to flow into the mindful dance. Be alert, aware, super-connected, able to create beautiful music, and a beautiful dance of vast possibility will begin to move within them.

6 — The conscious mind

There's a song that we're all singing and it's a song of possibility for the whole of the human race. But it isn't until you "hear the music" that you can touch and tune into this limitless possibility.

As you coach others, get comfortable with the movement of potential and be adventurous in discovering knowing in the living mind, beyond polarity to paradoxical creation.

Exercises

In polarity there is limited possibility—everything is either right or wrong, black or white, good or evil. In the past our world occurred in polarity because we were in a closed energy system. Today, our open energy system gifts us a paradoxical reality, one in which all truths can be true and a variety of perspectives can apply in every situation. Limitless possibilities now abound for each and every one of us and it's simply about being open to discover the ones that empower the moment for you and others.

· **Enable limitlessness through your thoughts and beliefs** – What creates limitlessness is the belief that it is possible. Consider that it is only the thoughts and beliefs of our brain-mind that limit us. Anytime you're feeling trapped or small, stop, expand and look at the thoughts you have about whatever it is that's come up. See if they're limiting you in any way and then see if in fact they're actually really true for you. Be aware of and alert to what really creates limitlessness around you. What captures your mind, boxing it back into a little box of limits? Start seeing, opening up and enabling limitlessness to proceed.

· **Tune into potential** – Set your intention to be aware of and in touch with the potential that will shift life in the moment. It's here that life really begins to open up for you, for your clients and for our world. It's here that we begin the journey into human evolution, creating that which has never been thought of or created before, making life more joyful, exciting, vital and dynamic for all of us.

EXPERIENTIAL PRACTICE: GETTING IT OUT THERE

· Observe during your day how much time you spend "in your head." Explore whether being in your head opens up possibilities and life for you.

· Breathe, relax and expand, moving into the Living Mind. Practice it with a client or a friend. Play with it, not just with yourself, but with others as well.

BREAKTHROUGH

We are evolving way beyond anything we have previously dreamed. New abilities are surfacing in adults and in our children that are offering us unprecedented possibilities. How can we use these evolving abilities to create new frequency, resonance and vibration for the new music of the human soul? How can we operate as a shared, open, living mind, sustaining our uniqueness *and* empowering our collective dreams?

The breakthrough of this chapter is knowing that the Living Mind is real, that it exists, that it is here right with us and can be moved into at will. The breakthrough is to discover that it exists, but also to discover that you are it! You become the Living Mind and from there, you source and create life all around you!

With the Living Mind, we can do amazing, limitless things. Anything we believe we can do, we can do. When we work together in shared mind or shared consciousness, we become part of an orchestra, discovering the rhythms of potential and creation, feeling into the energy of what wants to be, and evoking potential through our song.

CHAPTER II
ACCESSING PASSION AND VISION

Intention Of This Chapter
- To access the pure and profound energy of passion and vision for yourself and for others
- To enable you to recognise passion and vision as it moves to and through you and others

Profound Potential
- To coach people to the level of profound motivation by accessing pure passion, the energy that inspires the purest action
- To open the door to limitless possibilities and to give you and those you coach access to living as them

Key Elements

1 — Passion as energy
Exploring the excitement that creates.

2 — Vision as energy
Manifesting potential into the real and actionable

3 — The journey into passion and vision
How to express passion and vision and live it.

4 — Evolving vision
Allowing vision to grow and evolve in partnership with you. Feeling the vibrancy and aliveness of passion and vision every day.

Exploratory Discussion
1. Where do you feel passion? How does the energy move? How do you connect to that energy?
2. What is vision and how do you connect to it?
3. What is the relationship between passion and vision?
4. What triggers the movement or change of a vision? What happens to us in the process of recreating a vision? How do you know when to let go?

ESSENTIAL CONTENT

1 — Passion as energy

Passion is an incredibly exciting feeling that bubbles up and through your body; with it comes the energetic movement of ideas and thoughts that dance in your cells. It makes you feel really alive.

If potential is the limitless possibility of all that can come from a moment, then passion is potential rising, the first movement of potential through our bodies. It is the fuel that drives vision into action. It is the excitement that creates.

Passion (which is chaotic, moving and exciting) is a movement toward vision. You can be passionate about anything—chocolate, scuba diving, cooking, dancing, and so on. You don't have to have a heroic vision for passion to rise. But without passion for a vision, don't even attempt to take it on because you will have no energy for it.

Exercises

The journey into passion and vision begins by opening up our hearts and reconnecting to what we love. As a coach, if you are moving a client through this experience, it is important to be passionate and to feel the energy of passion. This energetically creates a space for passion to be and enables others to access theirs. It is synergistic—as you get yours, everyone else around you is lit up with theirs.

· **Bring up the emotions** – Ask yourself or someone you are coaching: *What do you really love?* When someone thinks of, talks about, or feels what they really love (i.e., are passionate about), their hearts open and the energy of that passion moves through them. That energetic movement lights up their eyes, quickens their breath, and they become more animated , more alive!

You can also ask: *What makes you really angry?*

Passion also lies underneath anger. Why would you be angry if you didn't care so much?

When you ask what makes someone angry, anger, as energy, starts to bubble up from the gut—as will what is underneath the anger (potential). Consider that anger may be the tip of potential rising. The task, as coaches, is to listen for what is underneath the emotion and to discover the true potential that's waiting to be found, explored and expressed.

To discover what is underneath anger (or any rising emotion), breathe the energy of the emotion up. But don't just stop with the emotion; bring up the energy that's underneath the emotion as well. Allow the energy to flow through the high heart (breastplate) and place it in the space in front of you. Now ask what this energy is. Get into relationship with it and all that it holds (potential). Talk to it, see it, sense it, experience it. Intend it and pretend if you need to.

- **The ocean of soul** – Another way to access passion is through a visualisation we call *The Ocean of Soul*. Imagine a water slide from the center of your heart winding and sliding down into the ocean of soul that surrounds you. You may feel this ocean of soul inside you or just outside you in the air in front of your rib cage and solar plexus. Picture a south sea ocean, sparkling in the sun. There you are soaking in the wonder of a wonderful sunny day.

As you look down at the myriad of colours and wonders on the ocean floor, you see bubbles rising from it. Dive down (yes, you can breathe under the water) and stand over the bubbles, allowing them to rise through your heart and high heart (breastplate), flowing through you into the air around you.

Get into relationship with the energy and ask, "What is my passion?" Commune with that energy to discover your latest, most passionate passion.

- **Where does the energy sit?** – Sometimes, people can not breathe the energy up and through. If they can't, ask them where the energy sits:

Where is that feeling of anger in your body?
What does it look like and feel like?
Does it have a colour or a sound?
Is it moving?
Is it static?

It may not be necessary to get it out of the body to work with it initially. Once the client knows where it sits, the movement of energy more naturally begins, bringing it more into their conscious awareness and getting them into relationship with it. Then you can help the client breathe the energy up more consciously. Ask them to place the energy in front of them and engage with it.

What is it?
What does it want?
What is it asking of me?

As the coach, you must tune in to that energy and communicate constructively about what you sense the potential as being. Have a dialogue with them around what the emotion is really bringing alive. Many times, people can feel the energy, but aren't able to label it.

- **Deep listen to find the energy behind the words** – To enable a client to access their passion, run them through the passion exercises in the Essential Content section. This should bring the energy of their passion more powerfully present. If that doesn't work, "deep listen" to the client's conversation around it. Listen beyond the words, beyond what they think they're trying to say. Listen for what it is that really wants to be said through them now. Sense what is really behind the client's words.

See if you can discover the thought or belief that may be restricting the flow of their passion energy. Often that thought or belief will be cultural, not personal. We have beliefs that have been shaped by our cultural influences and we have no idea how much they shape the very nature of our lives. These beliefs may not even be a true thought or belief in this moment for that person.

Once you've discovered the thought or belief that is restricting the flow, look together to see if it is actually true for them now. You'll likely discover that it is actually no longer true for them, and that being the case, the thought dissipates and the energy of their passion begins to flow again.

If you want to go even deeper, tune in and listen for the energy behind the words. Listen for what is really happening in their passion field. A passion field is like an artist's palette of different passions to paint life with, and yes, we can have multiple passions! Once you're in touch with their passion field, speak from there the words that will bring the passion alive. Allow yourself to be a part of their passion and then the right words will come through you to stir it within them.

Listen for the bubbles of movement, joy, vibration, bliss, excitement or any other energetic clues that will give you the signal that passion is moving.

When you feel it in the client's voice, you energetically begin to co-create the passion dance with them. The key here is to listen with the whole of you. It's like every single cell within you and around you has antennae standing up, paying attention, being aware, listening and actively seeking the way for the passion to emerge. Every aspect of you—your head, heart, spirit, soul, all of you—is listening. You're listening for the slightest feeling, the slightest change in the energetics of that person, so that you can articulate it for them to bring it more into reality. As you and they speak it, so it becomes.

2 — Vision as energy

Passion allows you to see and get excited about all the different potentialities of a moment, situation, company, or person. From there you can choose the specific aspects that stoke your vision. Then, you can bring those potentialities into the light of day, by focusing on your vision, partnering with it, and beginning to make it real.

Vision is potential waiting to move into play, waiting to be made real. It is the articulation of potential, of what can come, what is possible, and what can be now. Vision gives potential focus, shape, and form. It is the manifestation of potential into more specific, actionable frameworks.

Exercises

Once the energy of your passion is up and available to you, step into into it.

- **What if?** – Ask yourself, "What if I had all the time, money, and resources in the world? What would I be doing?" This will often unfold true vision and allow the energy to free flow. Often it's our inability to see it happening, that keeps us from beginning to really create the dream in reality.

- **Ask what it wants** – Ask the energy of your vision what it wants you to do. Once you've become it, you may get a slightly different answer for what your vision is, than when you were merely thinking of taking it on. If it is really yours, then embrace it— love, eat, and sleep the vision. Allow it to permeate every cell.

- **The ocean of soul (level 2)** – Imagine yourself back in the ocean of soul where the bubbles of passion rose through. Stand over the bubbles again and see that the crack through which they're coming is beginning to get bigger. A fissure opens up in the ocean floor. Dive down through that fissure, notice that it is light and airy down there.

    Discover there the storehouse of creation, an immense, sparkling cavern of all possibilities. Stand in this place and call to you the possibility, the potential, the vision that wants to happen through you now and that matches your passion, abilities, and intentions. Breathe the energy of this vision up and through your high heart (breastplate), placing it in the air in front of you.

    Now, ask what this energy is and discover what you can of it. Once you've done that, choose whether or not you'd like to partner with this vision. If you decide yes, then step into it and say YES to it as a partner, a steward, a champion, and a leader for it.

(NOTE: It's fine to say no also, but know that doubts about a vision are usually cultural, derived from limiting belief systems, and not necessarily true. You can choose to step away from thoughts and limits and say, "Yes, this makes my heart sing. I can do no other" or "No, it's not for me; I'd like something else.")

Create a profound relationship with the vision. Make sure to have the experience of stepping into the energy, because you'll find that you'll then walk in an energy field that is far greater than your own. In this partnership and in this expanded and refueled energy field will come all manner of synergy and synchronicity that will support your vision moving vibrantly into the world.

- **Tune in with your whole being** – Try accessing a client's vision without any spoken language being used. First, tune into their essential vision or what wants to come through them now. What is it that they may not be aware of? The skill is to completely trust yourself in the tuning in and seeking process. Close your eyes, stand back, be with the person's energy (i.e. tune in), sense that energy and search out what part of it is their contribution to the world (i.e., their vision).

Begin by intending to tune in. Focus your intention to access the vision, what wants to happen through them now. Your whole body and energetic sensors will tune in because you have intended it.

Step into your own heart, soul, and wholeness and meet them soul to soul, whole to whole. Evoke your soul connection. When you do, you will feel profoundly connected to that person and probably even more connected to yourself. You are likely to feel warmth and a precious closeness.

Expand your energy field and intend to move into a 'clear space.' This is a space in which you allow yourself not to know, in which you give space for what's right to know to arise. You might hear words or see pictures, symbols, or colours that will give you insight into what the person's vision is. Whatever you get, you can ask more questions to learn more about it. Share this process and information with your client in order to deepen the conversation around what their vision really is and how it can unfold.

Ask the question inside yourself, "What is their contribution for the world, their profound vision?" You will get a sensation of "knowing." It can come in many forms. Allow "it" to come, whatever "it" is. Knowing generally comes very fast, so be prepared to allow the knowing to absorb into you and catch it energetically, then bring it up so you can translate it into the mind and into language that you can understand.

Trust that which comes and communicate it back for an unfolding conversation for the realisation of their vision.

3 — The journey into passion and vision

Passion, potential and vision are energy that move, flow and dance through you, others, and the world. Given this is energy, we can be in charge of its flow.

Exercises

Walking as the energy of your passion and vision, listen to what comes up in order to discover what wants to happen next.

· **Get wild** — Give yourself permission to get wild with and to fully and totally partner with the energy of your passion and vision. Allow it to carry you away.

· **Begin conversation with it** — Help it become a reality through language and com munication. Talk to people about it. Get them involved by listening to you talk about it and by participating with it. Get ideas.

- **Look for signs** – Be alert and aware at all times as to what is happening around you. In every touch of the wind, in every word of a song, and even in a car passing by on the street, you will see signs of the vision communicating with you. You will begin to see how things are altering to meet your vision. The vision will become clearer through this guidance process and if you allow yourself to be guided by it, you will discover that momentum is beginning to fuel the creation process.

4 — Evolving Vision

It used to be that vision was a lifetime thing—your one life purpose, destiny, or raison d'etre. But today, vision moves rapidly and quickly into play. Working in the open, living mind, vision becomes fluid, dynamic, ever-changing, and evolving. Be prepared to discover an amazing and exciting vision one day and to have it change the next, but not because you're lurching from one thing to the next, but because you may actually have done your work in relation to that potential.

Exercises

Allow vision and potential to have a life of its own, growing and evolving in partnership with you.

- **Partner with it** – Continually partner with the vision as it changes and evolves. Consciously choose to become your passion and vision and consciously say, "Yes, I want to play, to partner with it, to express it, to live it and to carry it on through." You will feel the energy of its movement because you're not only partnering with it, you are it.

- **Surrender** – Once you've partnered with it fully, then relax and allow the vision to take you where it needs to take you. Allow it to light up your life. Let go of trying to move it in a certain direction; instead, move graciously and lightly with what wants to happen. If you really want to link to the higher, deeper, purer levels of passion, potential and vision, you have to let them work through you without controlling them. Enable your passion and vision, live it, breathe it, speak it, write it, be it.

EXPERIENTIAL PRACTICE: GETTING IT OUT THERE

- Just for a moment, drop the vision you currently hold for yourself. Focus on breaking through: What is that bigger, more profound, more universal, more empowering vision, that is bigger than you, that you would like to partner with?"

Try going global or even cosmic in your view. Play with it and see how it feels to you. Ask the question, "Does that resonate for me? Does it fit who I am and who I want to be?" If yes, step into it and partner it.

Next, live it, see it, breathe it, speak it, ride it. Observe how everything magically changes around you in a dance with and for the vision. Notice if a much more profound life begins to emerge for you and your work and play.

Allow the vision to evolve as it wants to without you trying to control or contain it. Remember to play, keep it light and easy. Discover what's possible as you move beyond yourself into a greater, deeper, bigger, more profound vision and possibility for us all.

BREAKTHROUGH

The breakthrough of this chapter is stepping beyond self into something greater than yourself. The major leap for us individually and for the coaching profession is to see bigger, to stand for the movement within human consciousness, and to work with what wants to be now.

Who do we, or our clients, need to be to be able to partner with bigger, greater, more profound vision? How can we do this effortlessly and empowered, rather than going in and out of doubt, fear or suspicion as so many people do? The breakthrough is to dive beyond soul into reality creation, partnering with the vision of what wants to be next and that matches with your passion.

This journey into passion and vision creates excitement and a sense of vastness, of tapping into something bigger than ourselves. Here we step into a much greater playground where possibilities are available that wouldn't even have been considered before.

This is where we coach clients to go beyond themselves to partner with a vision that is not just for them, but for more than them, for others or for all. This is where we coach others to discover what vision and potential is available for the world itself and beyond!

CHAPTER III
COACHING POSSIBILITIES

Intention of this Chapter
- To use possibilities and probabilities to consciously create the life experiences we want to create right now.
- To understand how to align and "true up" with the possibilities and probabilities available in every moment.
- To know where to find possibilities and probabilities.

Profound Potential
- Full empowerment through the knowing that we create our own reality.
- Being completely true while simultaneously being completely open, balanced, and excited.
- Creating the moment in every moment.

Key Elements

1 — Knowing
What are possibilities and probabilities

2 — Seeking
Where can you find possibilities and probabilities?

3 — Partnering
How to partner with the possibilities and probabilities of life.

4 — Coaching
How to coach another to see, sense, and feel the possibilities and probabilities of life.

5 — Communicating
How to responsibly present what you see and sense as possibility and probability in a coaching conversation.

6 — Consciously creating
How to realise possibilities and probabilities into life.

Exploratory Discussion
1. How do you define possibility and probability? What is the difference between what you already know as possibility and probability and what you don't know?
2. What does the discovery process feel like?
3. What does it feel like when an idea connects with you? How do you know it is connected? Do you feel it in your body, and if so, where?
4. Where do you go to look for the things that you and your client don't know yet?

ESSENTIAL CONTENT

1 — What are possibilities and probabilities?

Possibility is what's possible, what could be. They are the ideas and concepts that are already moving into conscious awareness.

Probability is the likelihood of possibility being made real. Probabilities are possibilities that are more likely to happen or to be easily achieved. A possibility tmay be more probable because:

- it suits you more
- it resonates with you,
- you have more energy for it and/or
- you see that it can be done and that you want to do it

Exercise

If a possibility is probable, it likely already has energy and forward movement. Getting in touch with the energy of it helps to determine that a possibility is probable and encourages its movement into reality.

- **Feel the energy** – To ascertain probability, feel into your connection to the possibility and its likelihood. How much energy do you have for it? Consequently, how likely is it to be achieved? If you have no energy for a certain possibility, don't take it on. Low or not energy is generally a sign that this is not going to flow for you, for others, and for Life.

2 — Where can you find possibilities and probabilities?

You can evaluate possibilities and probabilities by playing with the passion and vision exercises from chapter two. These exercises call the energy of possibility present, allowing you to see and sense the passion and vision around it, and allowing you and the client to determine how probable it is. Passion is the fuel that can move possibility into probability. Vision is the power energy that embraces the overall content, purpose, and movement to bring real clarity to the journey of exploration.

Exercises

If you already have a vision and you want to expand into further possibilities and probabilities, begin to open up to them. Take a deep breath, expand, and open to the energy of what comes up as a possible and probable. They may seem to appear out of the air or from deep inside you. Don't judge anything at this point. You're on a journey of exploration of possibility.

Play with openness in a variety of situations and discover all the various places possibility can arise from. Get creative and inventive with ideas of what could be. Don't try to invent them inside your brain. Allow them to pop up or in as if they were just waiting for you to open the door to them.

· **Ask what the energy wants** – If you're already in touch with a vision, you could ask the energy of the vision itself what possibilities exist for it. Remember to do this from an expanded state.

· **Sense each possibility's probability** – You may find that you have five to six strong possibilities. It's okay to have more than one. But what is the probability that a certain possibility will be realized? You can feel the answer. You can sense the percentage likelihood or use a scale of 'nil, low, medium, high.' This will give you a good sense of where the best choices lie.

Probability has a specific sensation of "this feels right for this specific vision and possibility." It feels like the percentage of possible manifestation is very high. It could also be measured against effortlessness, joy, or adventure. Is it challenging or inspiring enough? It could also be measured by power – how much power does it hold?

· **Ask 'Does this possibility want to happen?'** – Feel into the answer. If you pick up something wrong (i.e., it doesn't feel right) or run into roadblocks (e.g. the energy just stops and will not move), you can work with this. It doesn't mean stop and give up. You can bypass problems in advance by sensing the pathway for resistance and then determining whether that resistance is coming from you, life, or something else.

Other important questions to ask are: Is this possibility for the greatest good for me and/or the world now? What has the most powerful calling or attraction for me and for all?

Once you've determined that a possibility really wants to be and is for your and our greatest good, then go to work on de-energising the resistances. This resistance will likely take the form of cultural thoughts and limiting beliefs. It is simply a matter of seeing what's really true in the moment for you and them and then releasing that thought or belief so that the journey of exploration can continue.

· **Follow the pathway** – When you get in touch with even one possibility, it can often occur with multiple pathways. There's a state of being that lets you recognise which pathways of possibility to follow easily and graciously without confusion. By recognise, we mean sense, feel and, therefore, know. Accessing this state is a simple move from your head into expansion (you cannot do this from your head) and from there, to suspend all beliefs or thoughts for the moment, feeling into the pathways associated with the possibility. Aallow yourself to move with the strength of the energy and follow the pathways that hold the most energy at this moment. Then unfold their meaning and purpose by asking for clarity and understanding around them.

· Once you've followed the energetic pathways through to clarity, you are in a position to make an informed, clear choice. You can now set your intention for where to go next with it all. Once you've ascertained enough clarity, choice becomes easy and is the natural next step.

3 — How can you partner with the possibilities and probabilities of life?

Once the pathways are in front of you and you have felt into the more likely ones, then you're ready to partner with those that resonate the most with you. Let's be clear about something so that you don't end up taking on partnership as a burden. Partnering with possibility is not a life sentence. It is an evolutionary dance. As in any dance, you can change partners and music at any time. And who knows? In evolutionary terms you may have accomplished all you needed to with it in that one single dance on that one single day or even for that one single minute. It's all very flexible, fluid, and exciting in evolutionary terms. Don't feel stuck with what you've said yes to, as that will slow down or stop the dance and the gracious movement towards its realisation.

Exercise

· **Partnering with possibility** — This can be done in several ways. The first would be like shaking the energetic hand of the possibility and agreeing to a partnership relationship. The second is more like becoming it. Either way, you make an agreement to take it on, to be its steward, champion, lover, its living expression, to step into its energy and say YES to it, bringing it alive and real.

4 — How can you coach someone to see, sense and feel the possibilities and probabilities of life?

Working with possibilities and probabilities can be especially helpful for clients who are feeling confused or going through major life changes. It creates an opening for you and the client to move the transition state from chaos into creation, from confusion into the beginnings of clarity. You can coach them to sense and be in touch with what is available for them right now.

When coaching possibilities and probabilities, it's essential to come from a position of clarity, what we call the clear space. As we mentioned in the last chapter, it is a space not of knowing but of allowing what is right to know to arise. Before you begin your coaching, breathe, relax, expand and move to the clear space. To do this you need to get out of your mind; don't think about what to do. Set your intention to move to the clear space, then expand until you feel a sense of clearness and clarity. It is the point at which the mind stills and expanded awareness is lightly and easily available to you.

From here, connect with your most whole self, your client's most whole self, and the vast intelligence (the Living Mind) around and within you. In this clear space, your awareness will be completely different. You will be completely with yourself, your client, and open to possibilities and probabilities. You may feel irrelevant to the process and yet at this point you are both the observer and the catalyst. We will expand on this paradox throughout this chapter and this course. For now, just intend to move to the clear space and experience it. Don't get caught up in your head about what this means. It is simply an experience as opposed to something you can think about and from this experience of clarity, possibilities and probabilities can be sought with great ease.

Exercises

- **Play with possibilities** — Ask your client to open up and allow the energy of creation to flow on through. Allow all the ideas to come without judgement or assessment for now. Invite them to play! This is not heavy, serious, and significant. This is about pursuing the joy and excitement of life and all that we can offer it. Have them bring the energy of possibility on through and let the energy inform them. In others words, bring the energy present and ask what it's for and what they can do with it.

- **Move into the clear space together** — Another way is for both you and your client to move together into the clear space to tune in to find out what the possibilities are now. Suspend beliefs and thoughts around what you or they can or cannot do. You have to be willing to be stunned and amazed by who they are and what they can accomplish. This creates the space for it to happen. Dive into this open, clear space of possibility together and talk about in free flow what is truly possible for them now.

- **Feel their energy** — How much passion does the client have for the possibility that has come up? How much energy is in the air about it? You can feel the vibrancy of energy on a measurable scale (e.g. 1-10 or high/medium/low) when a person says "I'd like to do X." Does the person have excitement about it? If yes, go for it. They may think it's a great idea, but if they don't have any energy for it, then they can be mistaken about whether this one is really for them or not. Also, watch your own assessment and judgment of whether they can do it and be sure you're out of the way in order to have them truly assess that for themselves.

- **Expand into partnership** – Now, they are ready and willing to choose and move. How can you coach them into partnership with the energy of it? Have them expand until they get as big as they can be. Then have them breathe up the energy of the possibility and place it in front of them. Get into understanding of and relationship with it. Then, when they're sure this one is for them and it feels right to you and to them, ask them how it feels? Are they ready to partner it?

    If they are ready to partner it, then have them say so and make an energetic commitment to the energy. *Yes, I'm the one for this! I'll do it! I am ready to completely become this possibility walking in life!*

- **Hold space for resistance** – There may be a point at which someone wants to partner, but doesn't believe that they can. You can help by coaching the shift. One way to do this is to let them know it's a choice, that what they choose to believe is a choice. Ask them to suspend judgement for a moment and step into the energy AS IF they were choosing it. Let them pretend like they already have so that they can see what it feels like on the other side of the choice. Often, this will simply and graciously bypass the limiting belief and allow them to partner with the possibility and become it now by their own conscious choice.

    Sometimes, people get a payoff for staying where they are. You can help them to become aware of the payoff to be even more at choice. You can work at stripping away cultural belief (it doesn't have to be a personal thing). You can hold the space for them over whatever period of time feels right for you and for them, knowing that they will choose at the exact perfect moment, knowing that it is already so on some level of themselves. Or it may be time to turn them over to a coach who is more where they are in this moment. That may be the best thing for them and for you.

    If you can hold this space for them as the coach, their choice will get clearer and clearer.

5 — How can you responsibly present what you see and sense as possibility and probability in a coaching conversation?

The degree of responsibility for presenting possibilities and probabilities when coaching is dictated by the reason you are coaching: To help others? To transform the planet? To evolve human consciousness? If you're there for just what the client says they want, you may choose not to present new possibilities and probabilities that aren't aligned with what they think they want. But if you're both in this coaching relationship for transformation, creation, and evolution, then it's your responsibility to present any and all new possibilities as they come up.

Exercises

- **Stay true to the energy** – Once you've chosen to work with possibility, it's imperative to be in alignment with and true to whatever is coming up energetically. Sometimes you speak it out loud and sometimes you are guided by it without necessarily saying anything about it. If the client isn't "getting" what you are saying, you can try rephrasing it. Sometimes a single word will get people stuck on a misunderstanding, and equally, a single right word can open it back up again. Do this only if it feels right to do in the moment. You have to feel into when and where to stop and when and where to keep going. You'll know by keeping yourself consciously alert to what's going on.

- **Coach them to leap** – If you have an agreement to evolve consciousness together, then you can move into gracious persistence with it. If you feel that they aren't ready to move at this time, honor where they are now, but don't give up on the possibility for the longer term. It wouldn't have come up energetically as a possibility, if they didn't have some relationship to it and some reason for it coming to them. Some people need a bit of time to adjust to new possibilities, while others will take the leap immediately.

   With regular possibility, especially if it's directly related to a client's individual passion and vision, they can take a lot more time to align and partner with it. If it's appropriate for them to take that time, then you can hold the space for them to choose in a gentle, patient, non-judgemental way. Work with them on their path to breakthrough. You'll have to decide, as the coach, whether or not this person is genuinely working towards a breakthrough and how much time you and they are willing to give to the process.

   As a coach you can also train people to take evolutionary leaps, to be comfortable with change and to work with transformation. This takes far less time. With evolutionary possibility, the energy will move on to whoever will partner with the energy now to bring it into realisation.

6 — How can you realise possibilities and probabilities into life?

The most important first step of realizing possibility is to partner with the energy, to step into it and become it. As we discussed in step three, you can ask the energy what is the first right step to make it real now. It's almost like you can feel the pathways in front of you. Let the energy guide you toward one or two and get a feel for and understanding of them. Next, let the energy expand into the state of evolutionary consciousness.

Exercises

· **Expand evolutionarily** – Feel yourself become bigger than the Earth and perhaps even bigger than the cosmos. Ask to connect with the energy and consciousness of those all around the world who share your passion and commitment for this possibility being made real now. Feel the movement in consciousness begin and allow it to flow to where it wants to flow now. Doing this piece of work in consciousness first is like 'greasing the skids', creating the space for everything to flow with ease and grace into living reality now.

· **Sense the synchronicity** – Now you're ready to see how the realisation of this possibility fits into your current visions and plans and where you may need to make modifications to move into conscious creation mode. The more action you can take now, the faster the whole thing will move. It's almost like the first action opens the floodgates of realisation and out pours all manner of synchronicity and synergistic opportunities for it now.

It's critical to realise a paradigm shift in thinking here. It used to be that we would say to someone "Don't take on too much too soon. Stay focused and do one thing well at a time." But today, that no longer necessarily applies. When you move into an evolutionary state, with evolutionary possibilities, you move into a hyper-speed, ultra-creative state where you can manage multiple projects very well. In fact, if you tried to do just one, you'd likely be bored and slow the whole thing down. We call this vibrant multiplicity and it's a key part of the evolutionary paradigm.

EXPERIENTIAL PRACTICE: GETTING IT OUT THERE

· Play with possibility in all areas of your life, from making breakfast, to interacting with people on the street, to taking a shower. Play with it from the moment you get up until the moment you go to bed. Live possibility in a light, playful way. Let possibility come up in the bubbles in the air. Imagine white holes in the air around you. Stick your fingers in one, toes in another, and your nose in yet another. Bypass the mind allowing living intelligence to communicate new and next possibilities to you.

· Take a project you are already passionate about and let the possibilities all come in the different ways we described. Write them down. Find the ones that contain the most energy and put those in front of you like pathways. Stand in the energy and see which one has the most momentum, the most movement that you can literally measure from feeling the sensations associated with it.

· Pick one idea and play with it, holding it for a day or two. Watch it and see what happens. If it's right for you, you may get all sorts of evidence popping up. The energy it brings up will communicate what comes next.

· Try working with possibilities with a client or a friend. Discover your own flow with it. Practice it and see what happens.

BREAKTHROUGH

Possibility is all about play! As coaches, we can free up people's ability to play in this energetic arena in ways they haven't been able to before. It's time to not take it all so seriously, but to be light with it, playing on the playground of life.

CHAPTER FOUR:
COACHING CLARITY AND CONSCIOUS CHOICE FOR EVOLUTION

Intention Of This Chapter
- To attain clarity for yourself and with your clients in order to make clear, conscious choices with ease, grace, and passion.
- To coach others on how to step into the clarity and brilliance that the Living Mind offers, using the understanding available there to simplify and amplify the process of creation.

Profound Potential
- To be able to make clear, conscious choices, regardless of the scenario.
- To know that you can do this for yourself and with and for others.

Key Elements
1 — Finding the clear space
What is the clear space and where do you find it?
2 — Accessing wisdom
How do you access insights, understanding, wisdom and perspectives from the clear space to gain new clarity?
3 — Consciously choosing
How can you lead yourself and others to brilliant, conscious choice?

Exploratory Discussion
1. What do you sense a clear space is and what does it feel like?
2. What creates confusion? What if you could work with confusion as possibility rising?
3. How conscious are your choices? What if conscious choice is actually a creative act for evolution?

ESSENTIAL CONTENT

1 — What is the clear space and where do you find it?

You may have had an experience of the clear space in the last two chapters, and now we're going to delve into it more fully, to offer you some versatility within it.
The clear space is uncluttered; there is no thought there. It is an experience of being very present in the now. The clear space gives room—without the clutter of thought—for information, wisdom, insight, understanding and perspectives to move toward you. From the clear space, you can begin an exploration of whatever it is you're trying to understand. It gives you room to play and to look beyond what you think you already know to what is, as yet, unknown.

Exercises

Accessing the clear space involves moving beyond the thought process of chaos and confusion. Here's how.

- **Breathe into it** – Breathe, relax, expand. Notice the edges of your conscious awareness—how far out does it go? One foot, three feet, ten feet, as big as your house, your city, the Earth, the cosmos? Keep allowing yourself to expand naturally from your centre until you reach a place where everything is clear.

- **Intend to move into it** – Step from your mind (head) into the Living Mind (the intelligence around and within you). Imagine your head is an observatory rolling back to reveal the expanse of the sky, the stars, and the cosmos. Then take a step out into it and become it. This movement normally leaves one feeling expansive, vibrant, energetic and clear. You have now entered the clear space.

2 — How do you access insights, understanding, wisdom and perspectives in the clear space to gain new clarity?

With choice often comes confusion, usually because there are multiple options or pathways. Confusion is the state of energy flux before you make a choice. Confusion and chaos are very high states from which "the new" comes into being.

What if you could work with confusion as possibility rising, instead of as chaos and disorder?

When you open up to the clear space in the Living Mind, information can come to you that will give you new perspectives, insights, understanding, and wisdom around a situation. This information can come in the form of sound, colour, images, words or pure energy. You must allow the information to come to you without thinking about it. Simply allow the energy of the information to flow to you. If you stay with the clear space, you'll discover an easy grace of understanding naturally flowing to you. It's like you absorb it and the understanding comes naturally along with the absorption.

> ## Exercises
>
> · **Set the intention** – Set an intention to find the source point of understanding of what's really going on and why. Then let the energy lead you to a fuller understanding of this situation's nature and purpose.
>
> · **Be curious** – Don't just sit back and wait for things to come to you. Be an explorer and navigate by your curiosity. Being curious doesn't mean thinking more about it. In this case, it means to set your energetic intention to pursue the energy from a curious orientation.
>
> · **Follow the energy** – Once you begin to receive insights, continue to ask questions and follow the energy. Don't rely on a single input. Let every answer lead to another question until you go, "Ah- ha, I've got it!" and clarity is achieved. When confusion occurs, the process of seeking insight in the clear space moves from a simplistic and linear one (e.g. one step or question following another) to a multi-faceted one (sensing the strength of the optional pathways and allowing multi-layered information to become available to you). As you seek clarity, allow the energy to inform your movement through the living mind. If you find yourself back in your head thinking about it, move back out again into the Living Mind and let it guide and direct you to the insights that you seek.

3 — How can you lead yourself and others to brilliant, conscious choices?

You can make a choice from a number of perspectives:

- From what you personally want
- From what others want,
- From what the world wants, and
- From what Life wants. Here is where you discover your relationship to evolution.

When others are making conscious choices, it's really useful to help them see which of these perspectives they're choosing from and why. The more consciously they can choose evolution, the more the whole is affected and moved and the more easily their own passions and visions move into play! It's really all about the capacity and energetic strength of the field.

For example, if they choose what they want, they're working with their own energy only. If they choose what Life wants, they step into the full partnership and energetic strength of Life to be able to bring it into realisation, to evolve. There is a lot more energy available to get the job done as they move through these levels of perspective.

Very often people facing an evolutionary choice are concerned about the people and relationships they might have to leave behind if they take a big leap. This should be looked at with the person so that they can make a fully conscious and clear choice around it.

First, let them know that if they hold themselves back or limit themselves from moving on in order to stay with someone else, that relationship will likely slowly dwindle over time because they're not living true to themselves and their contribution to Life.

Second, the world, including their partners, family and friends, will all be better off and move forward further and faster for each and every one of us that makes the step.

Third, perhaps it's best to look to see if this partnership/friendship really does nurture and support the person in their growth. Occasionally, it is better for the person to take the step and move on. But more often, once they become who they really are, their relationships actually improve and take on a new depth and meaning.

It's your job as a coach to walk clients through this exploration into the possible impacts and benefits of their decisions and choices. Your job is to get your clients to see their choices in complete clarity, so that they can make a fully conscious choice that will be the best for them, others, and Life. You will have to be impeccably clear so that you can help your clients see through the fog. Don't enter into their muddle. You have to speak clearly and truthfully to guide them through it. The coach has to be willing to go beyond self and be the guide for the journey into conscious choice.

Exercise

- **Coaching resistance into the clear space** — Ask what thought might be stopping you or or your client from accessing it. Take what comes up first and see if that thought is actually true in this moment. Also, be willing to look underneath the first thought for additional ones that actually hold the power to keep you or them from clarity and movement. There might be a bigger picture going on that isn't available for understanding yet. If that's the case, relax and know it just might not be time to choose yet. Don't judge yourself if you or they can't get there. Relax, let it be a journey to explore.

When you're coaching someone to make a choice for evolution, it may seem to them like that's too huge a responsibility, obligation, or burden. But the truth is that in the evolutionary paradigm, everything happens with ease, grace, synchronicity, and fun. It's like the cosmos steps in to support you making it real. You need to be mindful for yourself and the people you coach of catching any old paradigm thoughts because they limit and stop the flow of the new into realisation and they don't really apply in the living of evolutionary lives.

EXPERIENTIAL PRACTICE: GETTING IT OUT THERE

· Put yourself in a space of doing something just for you. Think of two choices you currently have and pick one. It could be as simple as which television show to watch next. Choose because this is the one that YOU want and for no other reason. Then do it (i.w., act upon your choice) and see what happens.

· Set your intention to evolve life through your very next choice. Take the same choice you used in the first example and from this new perspective, feel into your choices to see if they feel any different. Explore the insights available from the evolutionary perspective and make your choice consciously—beyond what you alone want—considering what will unfold and evolve Life now. Again, take action on your choice and see what happens. Is the outcome different from when you chose it just for you? If yes, how and why?

· Find someone who's willing to play with you around clarity and conscious choice and practice this with them. Coach that person in making a conscious choice for evolution and see what you and they discover in that dance.

· Continue to play with your own conscious choices and become aware of what dictates and fuels them. Play within the evolutionary paradigm by making conscious choices for life and for the evolution of us all. Discover what wonders this will bring your way!

BREAKTHROUGH

The purpose of this chapter is to enable conscious choice and the conscious realisation of possibility, potential, passions and visions. Our intention is to move beyond the thought process of chaos and confusion to discover clarity and conscious creation. Why is this important? People are often confused and disoriented when "life happens to them." They tend to see challenging situations as complex or difficult. In this chapter, we look at how to evoke clarity in order to coach ourselves and others to make brilliant, conscious, and evolutionary choices. Evolutionary choices occur with a new strength, excitement, and movement that aren't available to us when we're choosing for ourselves alone. That is because conscious choice from and for evolution alters the whole paradigm (the energetic reality) in which we live our lives. The breakthrough of this chapter is the creation of a new paradigm in which the very nature of choice, and its pursuant action, is supported by the cosmos and ALL—in which the energy of ALL is made available to us.

Get ready to dance with:

· **Synergy and synchronicity** – A conscious choice for life, for evolution, more powerfully supports the fulfilment of intention. Inside this paradigm, choice may initially appear more complex as more options (possibilities) become available. What is actually happening is that more you are sensing into new possibilities that may more fully support your conscious intentions. Through synergy, synchronicity, and the attraction of resonant others, you find new ways to make it happen that you would have never have even thought of. The key is actually in a sense of detachment from how it actually gets accomplished, but a complete sense of rich intention to make it so.

- **Accelerated change** – In this new paradigm, what you choose today may change tomorrow—because that's the nature of evolution. Everything speeds up and can get accomplished in record time. Be willing to live in completely new ways and to allow everything to astound and amaze you with its ease, grace, and rapidity.

CHAPTER V
COACHING BALANCE AND FLOW

Intention Of This Chapter
· To access the profound state of alignment and balance, to be in a flowing dance with creation.
· To redefine balance and flow in the evolutionary paradigm, to source balance and flow rather than just following along with it.

Profound Potential
· To move from static, linear balance to dynamic, vital, fluidity and flow.
· To seek and source the waves of change, creation, and evolution, riding them with great delight.

Key Elements
1 — Defining the new fluid, flowing balance
Sensing the difference between balance as we've known it and fluidity and flow as we are creating it.
2 — Finding this new state
Connecting to it, staying in it, and, consequently. discovering fluid, dynamic equilibrium.
3 — Coaching the excitement of discovery
Helping others to feel the profundity, beauty, and inspiration that this space invites.
4 — Allowing and sourcing
Understanding the difference between the two and when each are appropriate to do
5 — Aligning and becoming
Stepping into what Life wants to be and becoming Life walking and realising itself
6 — Partnering the waves of change, creation, and evolution
Calling them forth from the ocean of possibility and riding them into being.

Exploratory Discussion:
1. What is the relationship between balance, flow, and creation?
2. How do you go beyond 'going with the flow' to dynamically sourcing the movement of creation?
3. What does it feel like to become the excitement of discovery?
4. Are you ready to be the source, creator, leader and champion for you vision?
5. Are you open to that something greater, deeper, and more profound that wants to be realised through you now?
6. What does it feel like to ride the waves of evolution?

ESSENTIAL CONTENT

1 — Defining the new fluid, flowing balance

Let's look at this as three distinct paradigms.

The first, let's call it 3D, is one in which you are pushed and pulled around and often thrown off centre (i.e. unbalanced).
    The second, let's call it the middle paradigm, is experienced when you are beginning to open to higher meaning and discovering connectivity and going with the flow. It is a good place to be, but it is still much more passive and stagnant than in the third paradigm.
    The third paradigm, what we call the evolutionary paradigm, occurs when you become the source and driver for what wants to happen now. You expand beyond self into a vast connectedness with all that is and from there, you can call forth the waves of change, creation, and evolution. Fluid, dynamic, balance occurs in the evolutionary paradigm.

2 — Finding this new state

In the new paradigm, you create the movement for what wants to be now. You become its source and its creator. You are more than just a passenger following along in its wave.

In the new paradigm, you are a vital part of the fluid, exciting, dynamic movement and you learn to find your balance inside the movement. It is this fluidity and balance inside movement that allows you to source, create, and evolve what wants to be now.

Once you're in that dynamic, fluid, balance, you discover that you're much vaster, deeper, and more connected to everything. You are more than just you. You are in relationship with everything that is going on. You are aligning with the whole and with what wants to be. You are stepping into a bigger energy and discovering a dynamic interplay, one that is much more powerful than simply riding the wave or going with the flow.

Exercises

Fluid, dynamic, balance occurs in the evolutionary paradigm and you access it through expansion. In an expanded space, you discover your relationship to Life, nature, universe, god, source, creator, whatever you prefer to call the forces of the cosmoses.

- **Going beyond 'going with the flow'** – Expand to the place of ALL and then allow your passion to meet the passion of creation, of what wants to be. As the two passions meet, a wave is created and something new is brought into being. The level of connec tion where this is made possible means stepping beyond the personal you and feeling your connection with what wants to be. When we coach people to understand their level of connectivity, they can then find, source and create their own waves of passion by getting into relationship with what wants to happen now and stepping into dynamic partnership with it.

- **Surfing in the evolutionary paradigm** – Surfing in the evolutionary paradigm requires energetic equilibrium. You must stay in relationship with the passion that is fueling the movement, and continue to dance in the dynamic, fluid partnership with what wants to be now. Ride the energy as it free flows through you. This is what we mean by fluid balance and equilibrium. More than simply allowing the energy to flow through you, you must learn to balance the energies that flow through you with the other energies that you're aligning to the flow. Expand and allow the energy to flow, but do not simply be its channel, act as its steward, champion, partner, source, and creator. Your job is to keep the power moving, to stay aware of the energetic flow and continuously source it and move it into realisation, until you're satisfied your part of the job is done.

- **Be the power** – Most people are comfortable with passion, but often dance energetically away from power because in the old paradigm, power meant control and domination. In the middle paradigm, power implies something external to you that you're seeking to understand and get into relationship with. In the evolutionary paradigm, you are the power for creation to realise itself. You become the source and creator for Life. Stewarding new power is like the feeling of being in love. When you embrace what you love and are aligned with what you're passionate about, then power flows through you. Stewards of true power in the evolutionary paradigm are discovering that they are passionately in love with Life and it shows up in everything they do. It fuels their actions, their visions and the realisation of possibility into being. This is true power. True power is what Life wants. It isn't personal. There's a feeling of rightness about it. It's strongly gentle—it doesn't push and pull—yet it is incredibly vibrant and vital, creating as it goes.

- **Coaching fluid, dynamic equilibrium** – show them how to:
    - move into the expanded state,
    - be in relationship with what wants to be,
    - align their passion with the passion of what wants to be,
    - source the movement of the energy in free-flow through them
    - align that energy with all the forces and connections that it requires to ensure its continuous movement towards actualisation

3 — Coaching the excitement of discovery.

Inside the excitement of discovery in the evolutionary paradigm, you BECOME the excitement of discovery living itself. As you become it, you forget all of life in front of you. But what if you're coaching someone who's not in the excitement of discovery? What can you do about this? You move into the evolutionary paradigm, into the exciting space that it offers, and then offer it out to those you coach to join you there. It isn't about meeting the client where they're at. It's about offering out the journey of excited discovery and getting them to feel the profundity, beauty, and inspiration that this space invites.

Exercise

- **Ask open, flowing questions** – To help someone move into the excitement of discovery, ask open, flowing questions like:

  Are you willing to live an extraordinary life and what does that look like?
  Do you want to find joy and vitality in all that you do?
  Are you willing to create your own path?
  Are you willing to redefine Life in every moment?
  Are you willing to live Life as a creative act?

It may be necessary to help them to understand that inside this paradigm, the discovery process occurs differently. It's playful, requiring a lightness of being. You may have to reshape their view of discovery from fearful or serious to playful, passionate and profound.

4 — Allowing and sourcing

Allowing is more supportive (you are lending your energy to the wave's flow) while sourcing is more leaderful (you are the energy that fuels and moves it). Sourcing is where you want to work from when you're taking on a big vision.

Allowing is a more passive, relaxed state in which you simply go along with the flow. You're quite attentive in this state to the movement and you move with it. Sourcing is more about you initiating the movement and then you ride it, steward it and champion it. Sourcing it is about owning it in a way that's different from allowing it. You take responsibility for fuelling it and realising it.

When would it be appropriate to use allowing and sourcing? Sometimes things want to happen anyway and you can't get in the way of it. Here, it's best to go with its flow. You'll know this by its feel—anything you try to do on behalf of it seems to be met with resistance. That is when you are being called to allow, to go with its flow. Alternatively, when sourcing something, you call it into being. You are the breath that initiates its energetic movement and it moves easily, graciously, and powerfully into existence. Additionally, there are moments inside sourcing where you do allow things to be. You will know when to source and when to allow. You are the vision fulfilling itself, so you are completely attuned to its movement.

> ### Exercise
>
> - **Coaching allowing and sourcing** – First determine the level of intention of the person you are coaching around their vision or project. See if they're willing to be its source, its creator, its leader and its champion. If yes, then assist them in breathing its energy into the air around them for realisation. If no, then find out what their role is with this project and have them move into relationship with it to determine their next movement with and for it.

5 — Aligning and becoming

How do we align with what wants to happen? And how do we align what wants to happen with our own passions and visions? Consider that what makes Life really move is not what you or I want, but what wants to be.

When we align only with our personal passions and visions, we can be out of sync with that which wants to be realised through us. When flow doesn't occur, it could be that we're actually out of alignment with the true movement of the vision. It's important if you hit this resistance point to open up to something greater, deeper, and more profound that wants to be realised through you now. It's important, in the evolutionary paradigm, to be willing to evolve what you're up to all the time. Why? Because the energy created by this movement is the power source of your vision's realisation. It's where the rubber meets the road and you really get things going.

In the old paradigm, you took on a vision and then decided how to move it into being. In the evolutionary paradigm, you BECOME the vision and move with and as its energy into living realisation. This is where the alignment comes in...you're aligning yourself to the power of the energy that's coming through.

You can take this to an even bigger level by becoming Life walking and realising itself. When you move into alignment with anything beyond your personal self, you step from your own personal energy field into a vaster, greater source of energy flowing, moving, and dancing itself into being. This is where the new power sources from and where things really get accomplished much faster and easier.

6 — Partnering the waves of change, creation and evolution.

In the evolutionary paradigm, you don't just ride the waves of energy as they move on through. You source and create them, both as they originate and as they actualise. This is the complete shift from *allowing* to *sourcing*, from *aligning* to *becoming*. You are the source. Without you, the wave may not move into being. You originate its movement towards actualisation and you steward its connection to people, places, projects, organisations, and consciousness for its ultimate realisation. To use the surfer analogy, you're not just waiting for a good wave to come by; you're actually calling it forth from the ocean of possibility to partner it into being.

There are different sizes, frequencies and forces of waves.

· The waves of change are more like light, easy, staccato waves. It's like when you're just learning to surf and you choose the smaller waves to practice on.

· The waves of creation are more tumultuous and frothy. They contain more power in them and they deliver onto the shores with a rush of excitement as something brand new surges into being.

· The waves of evolution are vaster, more powerful, and more sure. They have a more distinct movement. They are not scattered; they head straight for the shore with a resolute surety that says, "Here comes Life!' These are the waves that practiced surfers (creators) give their lives to in complete partnership. The surfer IS the wave and the wave IS the surfer.

Exercise

· **Partnering the wave** – Sometimes you may call a wave, but it either recedes sooner that you think it should or it won't come to you at all. When this happens, ask, *Is this want wants to be now or is this what I want?* Another important question to ask is *Am I complete now with my part with this wave?* The waves come out of what wants to be now and sometimes they and you can complete in one simple breath. Don't expect the waves of evolution to operate at all like the waves of change. They have a mind of their own' and occur in a brand new paradigm of evolutionary reality. In other words, while change may be slow and take time, evolution doesn't. It can happen in a blink of an eye and Life is forever magnificently altered. That's the joy of sourcing evolution. Waves of creation, dip and dive just like real waves. They are not always rising up to a crescendo. Sometimes there's a lull or moment of stillness while the next movement is gathering momentum. When this happens, tune in to see if now is a time to allow, to be with where it is without forcing the next step too soon. Be aware that this moment of stillness before the momentum may be crucial to its ultimate perfection.

EXPERIENTIAL PRACTICE: GETTING IT OUT THERE

· Imagine yourself surfing a wave and feel how that feels. Assimilate the power of the wave within yourself. Become its movement. This will give you a sense of being in relationship with the energetic power.

· Take a vision that you're currently at work on and see how you're aligned with it. Is it what you want, what someone else wants or what wants to be? See if you can step from what you want to sensing what wants to be along. If that feels right to do, make that alignment now and see how it feels to become the vision. If it's so right that you want to make it more permanent, then partner with it and become this vision walking. From there, as the vision, see what next steps want to happen now. Aligning in this way should take your project and vision into much more flow and momentum.

· In your coaching, be conscious of when your clients are in alignment with or in flow with what wants to happen versus what they want. Watch where the sticking points are and use this method of aligning with what wants to happen to unstick them and get them back into the dynamic flow of what wants to happen now.

· Explore the energetic movement of your own and your clients' choices. How does it feel in each moment? Is the wave rising or dipping? What feels right to do in your relationship with the wave to that as its source, creator and partner?

BREAKTHROUGH

Think of balance and flow as we've related to it in the past as static and passive. You are going along with what's already there, with what's already moving. Balance in the old paradigm meant that you moved to align with what already was or is. Think of the middle paradigm like surfing a wave; you are riding a wave that is already in existence. Now, in the evolutionary paradigm you are the one calling the wave into being and partnering with is as you and it evolves. But you are not imposing your will upon the wave. Rather, you are reaching into the vast oceans of possibility to call forth and partner a wave of potential into creation, into realisation. This is the breakthrough: moving beyond self to truly source, create, and evolve what wants to happen now.

CHAPTER VI
COACHING ALIGNMENT THROUGH ESSENCE

Intention Of This Chapter
- To learn how to align yourself and others with essence, passion, and what wants to be.
- To discover the pure clear space of living aligned.

Profound Potential
- For alignment to become a natural state of being.

Key Elements
1 — Opening to alignment and discovering your essence
Getting in touch with your energy and the flow of it
2 — Coaching alignment and resonance
Meeting and honouring their essence with your essence
3 — Aligning with what wants to be
Allowing the energy of ALL to flow through you

Exploratory Discussion
1. Do you feel aligned with yourself? If not, where is the feeling of non-alignment?
2. How do you experience another's essence?
3. What does the Living Mind want to happen now?

ESSENTIAL CONTENT

1 — Opening to alignment and discovering your essence

Alignment is living true to your essence. Who you are can dance and change over time, but your essence tends to hold a consistency.

What is essence? The dictionary definition is "the inner distinctive nature of anything or the qualities that make any object what it is." In a more spiritual representation, essence would be an aspect of soul that you uniquely represent. It is the fabric of what makes you unique. It is the pureness of you. It is your imprint. Every person's essence is different from every other person's.

Once you've got a handle on your essence, once you're in touch with the energy and flow of it, then everything aligns and falls right into place. You align with yourself, with your potential and with your biggest, vastest purpose. Standing in the wholeness and pureness of essence, you then dance passionately and powerfully into everything you do because your essence leads the dance.

Living in alignment creates a clear, true space for energy to flow through you and beyond you freely and completely from source to expression. There is a vibrancy and clarity in this state that brings about authenticity, integrity, and courage.

Alignment is about living whole and holistically. You are in alignment when you are being true to yourself, others, your environment, and ALL.

Aligning is an energetic experience. It feels like all the restrictions disappear and all the energy moves, flows, and dances into the wholeness of you. Then you discover yourself as a point through which creation flows. There's a lightness and an exuberance that comes along with this movement of creation through you.

Alignment moves you from a mind-body experience of life to a Living Mind-Body experience. From this aligned, holistic, creation space, you feel really good. Everything flows brilliantly. But if you make a conscious choice or conscious movement that's out of alignment with the true you and with the energy flow, you will begin to experience a sense of discomfort. You and the energy go out of sync. It can't flow through anymore.

Exercise

- **Opening to alignment** – Stand tall with your shoulders back and feet apart. Breathe, relax, expand. Really, this is about getting back to the essential you. Essence isn't some part of you. It's all of you. The parts are simply various expressions of your essence realising itself. So to become whole, allow all the aspects of your essence to flow into a rhythmic dance, into resonant alignment with one another. Feel the whole of yourself being present. Get a sense of expansion from the inside out. Allow the inner you to flow through and around you. There's a tiny inner core inside most people into which they stuff their souls in order to keep them safe and secure from the big harsh world. But this constriction of the core doesn't allow the energy of passion and vision to flow.

When you flip the soul out into living reality, you expand the inner core, making room for the flow of energy to move on through you. You automatically align because you have a bigger core through which all of you—and more—can flow through.

· **Realigning oneself** – Suppose you've been thrown out of alignment by an external event. Breathe, relax, expand, and allow the inner core to expand through and around you once again. Explore where in your body is the energy not flowing through. Once you find that point, put your finger on it and gently touch it like an acupressure point and then, simply allow the first thought to come up as to what is inhibiting the flow. Don't judge this thought, just take it as it comes no matter how silly or unlikely it seems. Once that thought is present for you, observe it and see if it's really true. If it is, then make a conscious choice to align yourself with it. If it's not true, press a bit more on the pressure point and allow the energy to release, moving on through you like a wave cresting on a beach. Give it no more energy than that. Then, find a substituting belief that empowers you and align yourself to it.

From this space, seek a greater, deeper understanding of the event and why it happened. In thinking that something external event happened to you, you lose the flow of you. But by understanding more fully what's happening and why *you* created it, reactiveness goes away and is replaced by learning, growth, and evolution. See if you can feel your energy flowing more freely around and through you now.

· **Discovering your essence** – The clues are in your passions. Your essence manifests itself in all the things you love to do. Look to your passions and see what fundamental thing they all have in common. Look to see what drives your passions, what's the source of them, and you'll discover a kaleidoscopic picture that makes up your essence. For example, one person's passions might be making music, creating art, or searching always for the newest new in the excitement of discovery. Their essence then could be creation creating itself. It encapsulates everything they are and do. Here's another example: A person's passions could be new learning, bringing soul to business, assisting others in becoming all they can be. This person's essence could be evolution evolving itself. Again, it encapsulates everything that person is about and for. Open your soul wide (flip the inner outer if it's not already out) and intend to feel, sense, and know the essence of you. Allow the energy to be with you. Breathe your essence fully in and become the living expression of it, of you!

2 — Coaching alignment and resonance

Alignment and resonance with another can be so simple when you are working with essence. It's only the fabric of who we think we are that gets in the way and creates non-resonance and non-alignment.

On the level of essence, we already are always aligned and in resonance with one another. Why? Because we're a kaleidoscope forming itself. All essences make up a beautiful holistic picture of the ALL. Once you discover this, there isn't anything you need to do but deep breathe and appreciate the moment of joyous discovery.

What is resonance? Resonance is when the frequency and vibration you're working on meets and attunes with the frequency and vibration of another. Non-resonance, or dissonance, can feel uncomfortable and even jaggedy sometimes. But resonance just feels right. It feels like two people singing the same song, allowing for different harmonies to meld together perfectly. You weave and dance into an aligned sense of wholeness expressing itself.

Resonance creates automatic alignment. When you are resonant with another person, there's a natural connectedness at a deep place. You make a heart-soul connection and your essence meets and honours their essence.

Exercises

· **Discovering another's essence** – Breathe it present. But it's not a normal breath, like breathing in and out through your nose. It's like smelling the most gorgeous flower. You're experiencing the smell, the breath through every part of your body, cells and being. Breath with your whole self and connect with another's essence through a sourceful breath. The discovery of essence is a joy. It's a profound experience to know who you and others are.

· **Aligning with another** – When you're coaching a client, it's important to be in resonance with them. You can do this by aligning with their intention and potential. You attune yourself to their potential frequency and then the two of you can dance it into being. You create the space for them to experience themselves by fully opening up and listening for all that they can be. There are cases where the frequency of another being or state of being can be non-resonant, in which case alignment may take more intention and movement on your part. Look at where you might be judging them. Judgement stops alignment. When someone feels discordant to you, get bigger than the situation and look to see why you and this person have called yourselves together. What's the learning, the growth, and the evolutionary potential of this moment? It's not that you have to work together to realise this potential. You only have to recognise the gift of this co-creation and move it into play. Then you can move on if you want to. You don't have to keep working with this person once the potential has been recognised.

3 — Aligning with what wants to be

When you're working with what you 'think' you want, you're probably working from your personal mind, from inside your head. But when you align with what wants to happen, you're actually aligning with the Living Mind. When this happens, the inner core expands exponentially and you align with the flow of ALL through you. This is a true state of power, creation and flow, which moves all manner of things easily, graciously and profoundly into play.

> *Exercise*
>
> · **Aligning with ALL** — Move your energy from your mind, and what you 'think' you want right now, to the Living Mind and to what wants to happen now. Ask the question, "What wants to happen now?" Intend for the energy of ALL that wants to be to flow on through. Asking the question creates the space for the energy to move and initiates the movement of the energy. Then it's up to you and those you coach to dance with it.

EXPERIENTIAL PRACTICE: GETTING IT OUT THERE

· As you walk around in life in the next few days, observe whether you are aligned with yourself, with others, with your essence and/or with what wants to happen. If you're not feeling aligned, come up with new, ingenious ways to realign yourself.

BREAKTHROUGH

Aligning with self, others, essence, and Life provides a level of energetic input that you may not have experienced before. This is the energy that fuels creation. The breakthrough of this chapter is to discover that alignment is a simple choice at any moment in time. You can make it a conscious choice and with that choice, connectedness happens and energy flows.

CHAPTER VII
COACHING CREATION

Intention Of This Chapter
- To discover that life is one big creative act.
- To source the new in everything you do.
- To be able to coach creation with and for others.

Profound Potential
- To unleash the powerful freedom and movement of living, coaching, and working as and for creation.

Key Elements

1 — Defining transformation, creation, and evolution
Moving beyond individual change to collective mega-possibility

2 — Choosing who you want to be
Reshaping your view of being human

3 — Taking the leap
Believing the impossible is possible

4 — Coaching creation
Connecting into the possibility for us all

5 — Lasering in for rapid metamorphosis and instantaneous movement
Opening up the energetic space for miracles

Exploratory Discussion
1. Can anyone access creation or do you have to be born creative to do that?
2. Is the sum total of your abilities and possibilities what you were given at birth? Are you who you were born as, with a pre-set destiny?
3. Is anything ever impossible? What is the limit on possibility?
4. What happens when you expect magic?
5. What if you are the source of all creation? What would you weave into human evolution that would offer breakthroughs for us all?

ESSENTIAL CONTENT

1 — Defining transformation, creation and evolution.

Change tends to be one step after another. It's linear. We start from "what is" and move towards something we think it can become. Change hardly engages possibility; it is simply moving a few steps forward or in a new direction. Change tends to be slow and sometimes challenging. That's because our culture has had a fair degree of resistance to change in the past. Everything changes all the time whether we like it or not, but in a closed energy system we spend a lot of energy trying to keep things the way they were. With hearts and minds closed, the whole of our own individual energy systems are not really available to us. All of that is shifting now as we move into the evolutionary paradigm. We are going beyond seeking change to engaging mega-possibility. In this new open energy system we can move into a passionate dance with change and discover the magical movement of Life.

Transformation is moving from "what is to "what can be. Like a caterpillar transforming into a butterfly, it looks like a miracle but what a caterpillar becomes is already written into its blueprint. Transformation happens more gracefully than change. Why? Because there's less resistance. It's a natural progression from one state to another. With transformation, you're not forcing anything. Transformation wants to happen and when it does, it's timing is almost always spot on.

Creation starts from a clean slate to make something brand, sparkling new. It's a sourceful act, a deep, profound process that comes from soul and wholeness. Creation is the whole of you moving into the Living Mind to discover the amazingly, wondrous movement of coming into new being. You are more than just a channel or a vessel for creation to come through. You actually instigate creation and source it into being.

Reinvention and creation are different movements and it's important to understand the distinction when coaching in the evolutionary paradigm. Re-invention is bringing change and transformation, bringing something new to what's already there. The essence remains the same, but it is enhanced or made different somehow.

So why would you want to work with creation as opposed to re-invention? Because re-invention is built upon the foundation of what already is and if you want to grant someone the true freedom of being, becoming, and evolving, then the best thing you can offer to them is the freedom to become more than they ever thought they could be. Our psychological culture would have us believe that we are the sum total of our experiences in this lifetime. Our energetic perspective allows us to realise that we are far more than this. We have all the learning, wisdom, capabilities and possibilities that we could ever yearn for, all within our own energetic make-up, right here, right now.

What if we actually aren't a series of qualities, abilities, habits, concepts, beliefs, and so on? What if, instead, we really are a clean slate for Life to write its imprint upon in every moment? Imagine the freedom to not have to be today who you went to sleep as last night. Coaching from and for creation gifts people this freedom to truly be and become whoever they dream they can be.

Imagine creating from ALL possibility, creating from creation itself, from that which wants to be created. Imagine creation partnering with you to bring something powerfully brand new into being, to let go of all that was and is and to start anew. It is fresh and powerful to have someone completely create themselves anew. It gives an amazing feeling of freedom as possibility rushes in. In this way, creation has a natural movement, an impetus of its own.

Evolution is when you take something and move it far beyond where it was, is, or can be. It's not even in the realm of known possibilities--it lies somewhere in the beyond. When you take up the reins of evolution, you take mega-leaps beyond what can be expected. But you're not just working on one singular thing or as one singular being. With evolution you're working on the whole and you're moving the whole into an entirely new place of being. Everything alters in the space that you create when you work with, as, and for evolution. What you evolve is for and from wholeness and for and from ALL-ness.

Of course, the question that comes up here is, "How do I know that what I'm doing for All is the right thing to do? How can I be certain that I'm evolving the whole in the right direction?"

These questions are easily answered in the evolutionary paradigm--in fact, once you're there, they don't even exist. You simply know what to do. You've moved beyond yourself and your mind and you're living as and for the Living Mind. From here, operating as and for the source of Life, you know exactly what to do and you actually can't do anything wrong from that place. You're connected and working with and for Life, so how could anything you do from here harm itself?

Change, transformation, and creation tend to happen individually, although creation can be done for the whole. But evolution is always collective even when you're just working with one person. In order to access evolutionary movement, you and the client become the whole and everything moves brilliantly into play.

Exercise

- **Starting with a fresh slate** – Assume you've just been born. There is nothing you've ever been before. You're a new babe and not even a new human babe, a new possibility emerging for us all right now, right here. Make yourself up brand new in this moment and see what you discover about creation and evolution.

2 — We are who we choose to be

We are who we choose to be. In this belief lies true freedom. It is the key to everything. We are spirit and soul, consciousness and creation, galaxies and cosmoses, wisdoms ancient and new, learning from past, present and future versions of ourselves and sourcing for all that is, can be, and will be. From here, all things are possible! If you believe this and can assist your clients to recognise its truth, then all the cosmoses are your oyster. You can literally become in any moment who you choose to be.

This belief begins with reshaping your view of being human. Are you just a human being in a physical body with set traits? Or are you the cosmoses dancing into Life? Consider that the physical aspect of you is just a tiny part of who you really are and can be. We're more than just the physical, but the physical weaves it all together delightfully. It's wonderful to access the freedom of creation in a physical body.

Suppose someone is shy. Were they born that way or did they become that way through a series of experiences in life? Did those experiences create a habit and then a self-defining belief about themselves? Is shyness a quality? Or is it an energetic state of withdrawing and withholding your energy? Could a shy person simply learn to breathe, relax, and expand in any moment when their self-taught shyness habit comes into play so that, magically, they're not acting shy anymore? Can you see that it's this energetic viewpoint that gives us the freedom to create ourselves anew?

If you believe that nothing is permanent and everything is possible, then what you get is a clean, clear space to become all that you want to be and more. We are infinitely create-able. We are infinite possibility.

Exercises

· **Play with your essence** – Describe your essence as you experienced it in the previous chapter. Is that who you choose to be now? If you could add things to the mix, what would you add? Or would you like to throw it all away and start completely fresh? Who do you choose to be now? What qualities, attributes, and intelligence do you choose to put in your new recipe of you? Expand into the energy of possibility and allow yourself to weave in the energies you want to become.

· **Call upon new energy** – Choose a quality that you wouldn't say has come naturally for you but is one that you really want to have. Create the energy for this quality in the space in front of you. Call the energy present then step into it. Sense it, feel it, be it, have it. Create this as the newest you. How do you feel now? How easy was this to achieve? Observe the movement that happens in your life now that you've chosen to become this new quality.

3 — Leaps: The impossible is possible

Impossible does not exist in the evolutionary paradigm, where we live in touch with pure potential and mega possibilities all the time. The impossible is only a limiting perception on our part. If you can hold the belief that possibility is unlimited and that the impossible is very possible when you take the leap from mind to Living Mind, then all of Life's wonders come forth to help you make it real.

Consider that "what is" can radically and instantaneously be changed, moved, transformed, and evolved beyond anything we've conceived of before. Use your imagination. It is the greatest creation tool ever. It bypasses the thinking mind and moves you and anyone else into the space of pure creation with great ease. It is actually creation realising itself! What you think and believe is what reality becomes. If ever you get stuck taking that next step or leap, imagine you have already leaped and see what it feels like. In truth, you will have just taken the leap; your imagination has allowed you to bypass your mind's resistance to creation. From here, you can make a conscious choice to remain in the clear space on a permanent basis or not. The thing is once you've imagined it, it's easily on offer for you in your energy fields.

Imagination brings impossibility energetically available. It calls all possibility and potential into reality. Our greatest creators and geniuses know this and create from this place. They do not live from what was or is. They live on the edge of all possibility all the time. They are co-creators of Life and all its magnificent possibilities. You can do this too. We believe that this leap into free fall and all possibility is easily accessible for any and all now more than any other time.

From the old, closed state, human beings existed as bodies and maybe a foot or two outward of their awareness of themselves and their connection to others, Life and the world. How could we connect with creation, potential and possibility if we were closed to it? In the past ten years, we have moved to an open energy system as our blueprint for the human system. Our hearts and minds have opened to the Living Mind and allows us access to and the integration of spirit and higher, greater energy, of the energy of passion, vision, ability, quality, intelligence, and more.

In the evolutionary paradigm, you'll find yourself always committed to evolution and evolving yourself. Therefore, creating yourself anew in any moment is a natural and fluid thing to do. There's very little resistance to it because you begin to see the total value, excitement, and possibilities that arise from creation. You actually begin to seek it.

Everything you need to know is available to you within the Living Mind. Don't wait until you're ready and fully informed to begin something new and apparently impossible. In living intelligence, everything is effortlessly and fluidly available to you. Again, you don't have to wait until you're ready and have the abilities you think you require. Instead, you simply begin leaping into the impossible and all the abilities you require to get the job done will suddenly and powerfully be made available to you--knowing, wisdom, innate sensing, telepathy, hyper-speed thinking, super-creativity and more.

You might think you have to get more patient or be more enthusiastic before taking the leap. The truth is that you could work on these qualities forever, but until you take the leap, it's just working on them, not necessarily accessing them. The qualities come with the leaping. Every person can have access to any and all qualities at any moment in time. That's the whole point of us being able to create ourselves anew in every moment.

We're not just suggesting here that you take a leap into what appears to be impossible now and again. We're actually suggesting that leaping become a natural state of being for you. What if you could live, think, and breathe beyond the conceivable? How's that for a life fully lived?

Exercise

To take leaps into the impossible you must be willing to move into free fall and ready to soar into limitless possibility.

- **Moving beyond the conceivable** –

    STEP ONE – Release, at least just for this moment, all thoughts and concerns of what's possible and what this is going to be like when you're done.

    STEP TWO – Breathe, relax, expand, move out of your mind and into the space of the living intelligence where all things are possible and made real. Feel the clear, clean space of possibility.

    STEP THREE – Become limitless possibility and see how that feels. From this place can you see that you can believe that anything is possible?

    STEP FOUR – Take something you're currently at work on, an idea, or project, or vision. Pop it into this pure, clean, clear space of all possibility and see what you discover as you move it and you into free fall.

- **Remaining open** – Some people have difficulty staying in limitless possibility because they are moving between closed and open energy systems. Every individual can choose at any moment in time where to make their connections: closed or open, mind or Living Mind, impossible or possible, limited or unlimited, and so on. It's really nothing more than a choice. Yes, sometimes we do find ourselves thrown back into the closed state, often automatically without having realised we've done it. If you realize this happening, re-open in order to reconnect to the limitless, living creation that surrounds us all. From this open and connected space, true movement can begin.

4 — Coaching creation

Most coaches coach change. As a reminder, change means taking "what is" and moving it towards something we think it can become. Coaching creation is a fundamental shift for the profession--it speaks to our role in calling forth profound mega-shifts for the people we coach and for us all.

Creation and coaching creation can only happen from the Living Mind. They occur in the place of mega possibility realising itself. You must enter into the dance with Life in order to bring them into being.

Coaching creation requires a shift from working with your physical senses to guide, lead, or move someone. Be willing to see those you coach as more than your eyes and ears can see and hear. It requires taking leaps into the unknown and dancing with your innate sensing abilities--breathing, knowing, creating, and alchemising exactly what needs to be done next to move Life forward. Be willing to be surprised at what comes out of your mouth and out of others' mouths. It is this willingness that puts you in the space of creation. When you expect magic, you get magic. When you're open for miracles, you get miracles.

Hold open the doorway for whatever wants to be realised right then and there in the session. As much as you're willing to to create is as much as will get achieved. When you're willing to see and hear beyond what they already are, when you're willing to go beyond their current potential, when you're willing to stir the very soul of creation itself, that is when you can truly coach creation and evolution.

Exercises

- **See your client beyond who they presently are** – Shift from working with this person as an individual to all the possibilities of who they are for the whole and for All. Know that holding a set of beliefs about your client limits how much they can create and evolve. You create an energetic box around them by the way you see them and relate to them. The more you let go of who they are now, the more freedom they have to become. This is a huge energetic shift. It ups the wattage, the frequency, the possibilities, and the energy; everything becomes more available as you free fall into this amazing space.

  Ask "Who are you relating to in this session?" Is it who they've always been, who they are now, who they could be, or who you and they have never even conceived of before now?

  Ask "What wants to happen now?" and open to the possibility that comes forth. Allow your imagination to soar. You'll get a different experience and a different outcome from the coaching session simply by asking this question. Why? Because what the person wants may not have all the possibilities in it. What they want is likely to be much less than what's actually on offer in the moment. Don't get caught up in what they are asking for and let that limit the possible outcomes of the session. Always ask what wants to happen at various points during a session and in future sessions as well. You can choose to do this consciously with them or you can do it on the higher consciousness airwaves. It's better to tune in together at the beginning of each session to see what wants to happen, but you may not always be able to do that with every client. Simply tune in and call possibility forth. Then if they're ready for it, whether you've talked about it or not, it will happen.

- **Coaching creation** – To coach creation, you must start with the present moment, without holding to any limitations from the past. If need be, work with your client beforehand to see how the past may be limiting them and to assist them in letting it go. You do this as an energetic movement without a lot of processing. In fact, we recommend you don't process issues in any way. Instead relate to this limiting past belief as energy and work with them to move the energy through into possibility. Now you can start from the clean, clear, open space of creation.

> STEP 1 – Ask your client, "What if from today you could be all that you've ever wanted to be and more? What if you could make yourself up from scratch?"
>
> STEP 2 – Create an alchemical space for them to totally recreate themselves. Visualise an alchemical pot in the space in front of them and ask, "What do you want in this new recipe for who you are from this moment forward?" (e.g., bravery, courage, honesty, openness, creativity, fun, lightness, joy, playfulness, profundity, depth, inspiration, love, empowerment, super-abilities, and so on).
>
> STEP 3 – Hold the space for them to become what they can't yet imagine, and also be the alchemical catalyst for the creation. In a way, you're the spark that lights the fire of creation by witnessing the creation. You have to be willing to see them as more than they can see themselves as at the present moment in time. You have the opportunity to gift every person you coach the freedom to truly become anything and all they would ever wish to be!

- **Coaching evolution** – This is about moving your client's creation and applying it to All for the evolution of All.

> STEP 1 – Move the clean, clear space you're both working into a mega space. In other words, move from your personal energy fields interacting to the collective energy fields of the human race (and beyond) interacting. This is where the magic really happens.
>
> STEP 2 – Be willing to go beyond yourself and your client to connect to the possibility that we as a race can be more than we've ever been. In that moment with your client, be willing to alter everything for everyone. An easy way to access this possibility is to understand that when you coach one person, you are actually coaching everyone else working in that same area and are able to move this breakthrough into play for everyone it touches all around the world. Simply setting your intention creates the right conditions for this energetic shift to happen.
>
> STEP 3 – Move the energy as it wants to move for evolution. It's not just about popping the breakthrough into the collective pot so to speak. It's more about you and your client becoming the collective and from this energetic space, the breakthrough occurs for you, them, and All. By agreeing to the breakthrough for the evolution of human consciousness, you step into a collective energy field that encompasses the world and beyond. Breakthrough is actually much more easily achieved in this bigger, mega space. Why? Because more energy is available to you here and it's powered by the whole, not just you and your one client trying to make something happen.

5 — Lasering in for rapid metamorphosis and instantaneous movement

In advanced coach training, you come on line for something way beyond what you've ever coached for before. You coach to accomplish in record time, huge leaps for individuals and for the whole.

Don't just settle for slight advancements. Be willing to totally and completely recreate human beingness and all consciousness in everything you do. Be willing to be a source for creation!

> *Exercise*
>
> · **Coaching for rapid metamorphosis and instantaneous movement** – To do this you must think and work outside of linear time. Be willing to believe that huge leaps are possible right here, right now for All. From this belief, and the energetic space it provides, you can do things you might have previously considered impossible. You may find yourself sitting forward on the edge of your chair, or even standing up expectantly for the huge breakthrough that is about to explode from you and through you. The greater energy puts you on high alert so to speak!

EXPERIENTIAL PRACTICE: GETTING IT OUT THERE

· Take a client, a friend, or a family member and play with them around the complete creation of themselves. Have fun inventing new recipes for living, for being, for playing, and for evolving us all. Discover the amazing movement within the space of creation.

· For one day, walk around as if you are the source of creation. Observe everything you do and everything that happens around you. Pretend that you can wave a magic wand and--poof--Life alters brilliantly and beautifully for All. Play with it and see from the expanded place just what miraculous creations you can design. What does that day feel like for you and what have you learned about sourcing creation?

BREAKTHROUGH

The breakthrough is becoming the architects of Life and coaching it in others. This is the new evolutionary paradigm and within it, amazing movement abounds.

CHAPTER VIII
COACHING ABILITIES IN THE LIVING MIND

Intention Of This Chapter
- To move from the mind to the greater, vaster intelligence of the Living Mind
- To learn to flow and dance with new abilities that source from that place of connectivity
- To discover breakthrough coaching in the Living Mind

Profound Potential
- To discover the magic that is available to us when we get out of our heads
- To fully align, expand, and step into the Living Mind, integrating it as a natural way to be where the connectivity is conscious and always available
- To be able to connect with others from within the Living Mind
- To discover that more than just being able to step into it, we are a source for the Living Mind

Key Elements
1 — Moving from mind to Living Mind
Expanding into limitless potential
2 — Accessing new abilities in the Living Mind
Intuition, wisdom, empathy, innate sensing, telepathy, bandwidth scanning, knowing, hyper-speed thinking, and super-creativity

Exploratory Discussion
1. Are you usually in the moment with your coaching, or are you trying to remember what to do? When you really feel connected to your clients, in the flow and in the moment, what is happening that is different from all other times?
2. How do you sense and connect beyond the traditional five senses? Where does the energy move to and from when you use these abilities?

ESSENTIAL CONTENT

1 — Moving from mind to Living Mind

In mind, the energy is more constrained, limited, restricted. All the energy and thought is inside the brow and the head. But when you move to Living Mind, there is a sense of effervescence—fireworks!—and expansion into limitlessness. You become All. You move beyond yourself, yet you are still you, just more of you than ever before.

You can do this consciously at will, but it can also occur spontaneously when you are passionately engaged in something that excites you. Then you can find yourself there without conscious intention. The passion flow takes you there. Your body feels easy and relaxed. There's an uplift in the energy, a vibrancy, and brilliance comes to you. You find yourself saying the perfect things for breakthrough to occur. Have you ever had those experiences where what you said astounded and amazed even you and the person you were coaching moved profoundly? This is you speaking a greater, vaster intelligence. This is the place that truly brilliant coaching occurs.

> *Exercise*
>
> · **Strengthening connection to Living Mind** — First, recognise what it feels like when you're in your head. Look at and sense where the energy moves. Now breathe, relax, expand and move to a whole sense of yourself. Then expand beyond yourself into the Living Mind. Intend it and let yourself flow there. Notice how that feels. Open the high heart (breastplate) with a breath. As you breathe outward, feel your "antennae" move into high alert and your super-connection move into play.

2 — What is available in the Living Mind?

As we discussed in Chapter One, everything is available in the Living Mind—all perspectives, insights, possibilities and potential. You set your intention for the "source" answer, insight, perspective, or solution for what wants to happen now in relation to you and your client. Then you allow the "source" information to move to you. Source information is the one thing that when we find it and speak it, everything else begins to unfold perfectly for the realisation of maximum movement in that moment.

Intuition — Intuition is a gut feel—you don't know how you know, you just know. You can use it in a quick situation when you need a quick answer or immediate guidance. It's a part of our natural guidance system but we've been trained over the years to ignore it. We believe that intuition is naturally available to everyone often, but people don't always listen to it or even acknowledge that that's what it is so it's a matter of choosing to pay attention to it when it comes.

Wisdom – Wisdom comes from reaching up and out for higher input, perspective, or potential. With wisdom, there tends to be more substance and content than with intuition. It will often come in more detailed format (e.g., words, sentences, symbols, colours, sounds, or a full running video). You use wisdom when you want a deeper, richer understanding and intuition when you want a quick fix. Generally, wisdom is associated with our learning of the past (ancient wisdoms), but new wisdom is also possible in the moment if we access the knowing and understanding of the Living Mind.

Empathy – Empathy is the ability to feel and experience another's emotional state energetically. One of the dilemmas with empathy is that you can energetically take on others' emotions as your own, often not even realising that you've done so. If you are going to use empathy, it's important to be aware of and in tune with your own emotions, so that you can distinguish yours from others. Empathic sensing happens through the solar plexus area of the body, which is the emotional centre. If you move this sensing ability up through the heart / high heart, it evolves instantly into innate sensing, which will give you much more access to what it's all about and for, while at the same time leaving you energetically clear (see below).

Innate sensing – Empathy is tuning into the emotion itself (e.g. pain, suffering, joy, etc.), whereas innate sensing is tuning in to the potential of the emotion. Innate sensing is holistic—you use the whole of you—to sense, feel and explore what is happening in the air around. With innate sensing, you have the sense of millions of little antennae moving to high alert to be attuned to what's happening and what wants to happen.

Knowing – Knowing occurs more spontaneously and in the moment. You super-connect into the Living Mind and all that you need to know is available to you there. As opposed to with intuition, you know that you know what you know and you know how you know. Knowing offers clarity and a fuller, richer understanding.

Telepathy – Telepathy is being able to read, sense, know, and understand the energy of the whole of a communication. We distinguish three levels of the wholeness of communication:

- language – what the person is saying in words.
- telepathy – what the person is really wanting to say. It's what they're sort of in touch with, but they haven't been able to get their heads around it yet to communicate it in words
- deep telepathy – what is really wanting to be said, the potential behind the words.

With telepathy, you listen with the whole of you to the whole of the communication and with deep telepathy, you listen from beyond yourself as All listening to All in and around another. With deep telepathy, it's not a one-on-one or personal conversation anymore. You're listening and speaking for what wants to be now.

Bandwidth scanning – With any situation, person, organisation, or moment, there are always multiple interpretations available to explain what has happened. Bandwidth scanning allows you to scan the layers (i.e., bands) of possibilities, interpretations, and meanings for these situations to discover what it's really all about and for. This is especially important to do when you have a client who feels stuck or if you yourself are feeling stuck with someone or something. You can get past the stuck point easily, quickly and graciously by finding the interpretation that frees them and you from it.

Hyper-speed thinking – Have you ever experienced having multiple ideas, knowing all about them and selecting one idea or perspective—all in less than a few seconds? This is hyper-speed thinking. Hyper-speed thinking occurs outside of time completely, so it actually seems as if everything is slowing up to give you all the time in the world to access the information, but only a few seconds has passed. We call this hyper-speed grace and believe it may actually be the natural state of our intelligence, but we've trained ourselves to play within linear time, thereby preventing the rapid downloads and uploads of full information that are available to us. Hyperspeed thinking is like when a surfer makes a snap millisecond decision to do the exact right thing to stay on the wave. It actually occurs for them as multiple inputs coming at them that they're able to sort through in a split second. They've trained their minds to open to Living Mind in order to transcend linear time.

Super-creativity – Super-creativity is opening up to all the possibilities of creation and allowing an upload or download of ideas and possibilities to flow right on through. It is a state of flow with All that is. But you're not just dancing with the flow. You are both the source of it and the partner to it at the same time. Like hyper-speed thinking, ideas roll on through in quick succession, and along with them will often come a rush of energy that can cause a lot of heat in the body (hot flashes) as passion rises. The super-creative state is an exhilarated state in which ideas seem neverending and are brilliant beyond compare! Super-creativity does have its own ebb and flow, so there are times when it will seem as if you can't access it at will. But there will also be times when you are completely in charge of its initiation and its movement.

Exercises

· **Accessing intuition** – Intuition is accessed by opening up your heart. The energy moves from the rib cage area to your conscious understanding in your mind. It's like a whoosh of energy from within you or from just outside of you to give you a signal for what to do, where to go, or what to pay attention to.

· **Accessing wisdom** – Wisdom comes from the higher self. You reach up and out from an open heart and mind to access it. Expand beyond yourself, get bigger than the cosmoses, and intend to have it. To access ancient wisdoms (i.e., what has been learned and placed in consciousness before), move your consciousness out into a giant consciousness archive and direct the search for what wisdom you wish to access. Alternatively, accessing new wisdom requires a creative process in the moment. In this case, you are its creator not its searcher. You are in a collaborative dance with what wants to be and without you it won't become. This is how the geniuses of our times operate. They access intelligence beyond known intelligence and bring into being new concepts that have never been before. And anyone can do this! It is not just for the intellectual elite.

· **Empathy** – Empathy tends to orient itself around the solar plexus area as this has been traditionally the seat of our emotional centre. Empathy is about sensing others' emotions. You are opening your own emotional centre to the emotional centre of others. We do urge caution here as this type of sensing can feel chaotic and unpleasant, and can result in you taking on the emotions of others. The question here is whether sensing, tuning in to, or taking on others emotions is valuable at all to the coaching or contribution process. Connecting with another's pain can give you a diagnostic tool for coaching and assisting them, but the pain is not the issue. Instead if you tune in to the potential of the emotion, you will find the whole experience much more valuable, informative, easier, and gracious for both of you. This then allows the transformation process to move rapidly into play. To see how this is done, read the innate sensing section which follows.

· **Innate sensing** – Innate sensing uses the whole of you, not just one particular area like the heart or solar plexus. All of your senses attune to the energetic state of all that is and can be. The millions of antennae that are an essential part of you and of the Living Mind move into high alert attuning to what's happening and what wants to happen. You're not just sensing the problem or the emotion, which is a denser, lower frequency, but the higher vibrational frequency of its potential. As soon as you get into relationship with the potential, the frequency shifts and true transformation begins. This is where the opening of the high heart is essential to attaining the state of wholeness and to attuning to these higher frequencies.

· **Knowing** – Knowing comes when you move beyond yourself into the full experience of the Living Mind. You become ALL, moving beyond self into a state of complete and full knowing of all that there is to know in that moment regarding your focus of intention. How does this differ from wisdom? You're not searching archives of consciousness; you are the living information.

· **Telepathy** – Telepathy is again achieved through wholeness and beyond. Telepathy generally focuses around the rib cage area of the body (both internally and externally) and translates up into the mind. It's as if you have energetic transmitters and receivers that send and receive information (energy). You are listening with the whole of you to the whole of another. You are opening up yourself to truly receive what another is really wanting to say. Then, with deep telepathy, you listen from beyond yourself as All listening to All in another. You are expanding yourself further to listen beyond the personal to see what is really wanting to be expressed, explored and created in the moment.

· **Bandwidth scanning** – Bandwidth scanning opens you up to a clear space where you can explore the various ranges or levels of possibilities, meanings, interpretations, and perspectives inherent in the moment. You reach out in front of you and begin to assess and explore the bands of frequencies and possibilities on each level, beyond what our cultural interpretation can imagine or our human brain can comprehend. Bandwidth scanning assumes that we are dancing to a greater tune, that there is a deeper, richer meaning to life as it unfolds, regardless of how chaotic it might look in the moment of its happening. So you look into the deeper personal and beyond personal to discover what that deeper, rich meaning might be.

· **Hyper-speed thinking** – To experience the hyper-speed state, expand into pure creation and pure consciousness. If you move into consciousness, you don't necessarily get hyper-speed thinking. In fact, like meditative states, it can slow down your thinking. But link consciousness to creation and you have an active super-creative conscious state in which everything occurs rapid-fire fast. Then to work in the hyper-speed state, surrender any belief that we can only think in linear time and in small bits of information one at a time. As you become the Living Mind, you allow the flow of All to come to you undisturbed. As the uploads (from the deep inner) and downloads (from the higher outer) come to you, your job is not to think but to simply assimilate and allow the knowledge to flow on through. Allow your Living Mind to do the job of thinking for you and in that space, you will discover how easy it is to move beyond time into hyper-speed grace and hyper-speed processing. But you must be willing to allow for the evolution of mind in order to access this. Surrender to it. It's more natural than you might think.

· **Super-creativity** – Open wholly and connect to the living intelligence. Then breathe deeply and intend to connect with that which wants to be now through you. Breathe it up and through and let the energy of it flood your body. Be in it and of it for a while, enjoying the partnership with it. You can even become it if you wish to; that would mean being ready to bring this one right on through. Now, from within this energy, ask for all the ideas and possibilities that come with this creative concept, idea, or vision. Don't think it. Just relax and let multiple ideas come on through, like in the hyper-speed state. Don't worry about remembering them or assessing them. Just let them come on through and sense your relationship to each one. There will be one or more which will resonate and you'll be off and running.

When you bring super-creativity into a group situation, the air is charged with new ideas. People come alive and they're bursting to share what's coming up for them and loving the movement of the whole towards something uniquely new. Getting a

> group to this state requires asking them to tune in to the energy of the potential and allow it to flow on through. Let everyone share what they get with no holdbacks, no judgment, and no commitment to having it happen. Record every idea so nothing is lost. Once the download is complete, everything will seem to fit together into a wonderful neat package, as if each piece was just waiting to come on through each individual to make up a kaleidoscope of creation.

EXPERIENTIAL PRACTICE: GETTING IT OUT THERE

· Recognise what it feels like to be in your head by thinking about something. See and feel where your energy goes. Look at your face in the mirror while you think about something. Then breathe, relax, expand, and allow yourself to make that shift into being the Living Mind. How does that feel? How do you look when you are in the mirror?

· Think of a situation (past or present) that you don't understand and try bandwidth scanning the various perceptions and interpretations that it can hold. Don't stop until you hit an "a-ha!" Feel the freedom that it provides from the upset, confusion, or misunderstanding.

· Try all of the various abilities out on a friend or on a buddy in the course. Play with them in order to strengthen the muscle of using each one. Remember, all of these abilities are available to us all, and the more you practice them, the better you become at using them all.

· When you're coaching your next client, be consciously aware of where your information is coming from. See if you can distinguish the difference between intuition, innate sensing, knowing, wisdom and telepathy.

BREAKTHROUGH

The breakthrough in this chapter is to discover your own natural ease with the abilities available to us in a Living Mind. By continually evolving our relationship and abilities within the Living Mind constantly we open ourselves and those we coach to a never-ending potpourri of possibilities!

CHAPTER IX
COACHING EVOLUTIONARY INTELLIGENCE

Intention Of This Chapter
- To evolve emotional intelligence and spiritual intelligence to evolutionary levels
- To be able to move freely into living, evolutionary intelligence
- To expand your coaching beyond mind and intellect into the dance of the Living Mind

Profound Potential
- To evolve intelligence
- To move emotion from issue processing to the celebration of emotion as potential

Key Elements

1 — Moving from traditional intellectual, emotional and spiritual intelligence into evolutionary intelligence
What's the difference and what does it feel like?

2 — Applying evolutionary intelligence to coaching situations
The best place for you as a coach to cooperate is always as connected to your fullest knowing.

3 — Assisting others in moving into evolutionary intelligence
The more you and they have trust it can happen, the easier it become.

Exploratory Discussion

1. In the past, when you've processed an emotional issue, how has it made you feel: bigger, expanded, shrunk?
2. What happens when you shift your view from problems to solve to potential to be realized?
3. What would it feel like to live in evolutionary intelligence all the time?

ESSENTIAL CONTENT:

1 — Moving from traditional intellectual, emotional and spiritual intelligence into evolutionary intelligence

Intellectual intelligence – Traditionally intelligence is associated with and experienced within the personal mind: intellectual intelligence. We absorb and retain information like a computer; it's a mental process that occurs in the head. Western culture tends to believe that when you're born, your level of intelligence is fixed. But what if that's not true? What if we can move beyond the mind, beyond intellect, to access new levels of intelligence that can take each and every one of us to new levels of intelligent living? As we move into these expanded levels of intelligence, learning becomes knowing and the entire process is transformed.

The brain is magnificent, but traditionally we've only used a small part of it for our intellect. On the expanded levels, we use our brains in an expanded capacity—it's like connecting your computer terminal (your intellect) to a giant mainframe (the living knowledge and wisdom of everything). The brain then functions like the super-brain it truly is, using all of its magnificent capacity.

Emotional intelligence – Traditionally, emotions have been undervalued, seen as reactions that need to be stuffed down and controlled. In recent years, emotional intelligence has grown into a whole new approach of being responsible for your emotions and being aware of the emotions of others in order to better communicate and connect with others. We are beginning to explore what our feelings can offer us in terms of personal and interpersonal growth. This is a great step forward, but it is still focused on the personal, individual human being perspective.

We believe that feeling is soul-oriented communication, that it's your soul (or our collective soul) letting you know that something new is about to burst on through. We can get to true feeling by partnering in a celebratory relationship with our emotions.

Our evolutionary view of emotional intelligence is that emotion is the tip of potential rising and that by reaching to the energy of what's underneath the emotion, we can discover the profound movement of possibility, potential, passion, vision and leadership available to us there. We begin to celebrate the emergence of emotion and partner with the energy of it to move Life forward for ourselves, others and the world.

What if emotion is simply energy in motion, E-Motion? What if e-motion is our body's innately intelligent guidance system offering us what's possible next—the next step, the next shift, the next potential? From this perspective, you are not constricted to just looking inside yourself for insight and answers. Rather, you are expanding and connecting to the Living Mind for your dance with emotion.

What's coming up for you through your emotions may not be just something personal for you. The energy of emotion rising may actually be your call to do a major piece of breakthrough work not just for yourself, but also for others, and the world? If we can get into relationship with emotion from this perspective, everything changes and the Dance begins! It becomes an exciting adventure where the next newest new is breaking on through. Yes, you are still completely and totally responsible for yourself and any learning that's on offer here *and* you are also working beyond self to steward the energy into play for us all. When you make a conscious choice to work for the world and for All, your energy moves in sync with that choice and places you in the energetic space where bigger breakthroughs can occur.

This is an incredible shift from the way we've always viewed our relationship to emotion. This view allows movement, which is the most important thing here. Instead of being frightened by emotion and suppressing or blasting it (or merely processing the energy of emotion from your personal perspective), you are breathing it out and through, celebrating it and working with it to maximise its potential in the world. To do this, you have to expand and be connected, giving you access to a greater you.

Spiritual intelligence – Spiritual intelligence is usually seen as the seeking of higher purpose and greater meaning. It's about the integration of the higher self, about seeing bigger and reaching up for wisdom and understanding. But spiritual intelligence is still about only one part of you reaching to try to understand something more than you. We want to evolve this even further where you're working with the whole of you for the evolutionary movement of the whole, the movement toward evolutionary intelligence

Evolutionary intelligence – Evolutionary intelligence is about living in connection with the Living Mind. It's about living whole, true, powerful and super-connected. It's about seeing the bigger picture of the whole and all. Evolutionary intelligence is our true ability to be a creator for Life, to be a massively capable evolutionary agent for potential to realise. From this place, we can evolve the very nature and fabric of intelligence itself.

What does intelligence look like when it's evolved and evolving? It occurs like a fluid state of constant, dynamic equilibrium from which movement sources. The Living Mind is constantly extending a hand to us, inviting us into the dance to be the source-creators of evolutionary movement.

We're inviting you now to become the Living Mind and from that place of being it, to evolve it beyond where it's ever been before. This is a choice. These are states you can move in and out of. You don't have to be it all the time, but what if you were? Consider this: What if human beings have been disconnected from their true evolutionary intelligence and power for thousands, if not millions, of years? What if this is our opportunity now, through every coaching situation, through every moment of our lives, through everything we do, to evolve the whole of living intelligence for us all?

Step from the mind to the living mind. Are you in it as you OR are you in it as it? Play with it and see how it feels and what you discover in the movement.

Exercises

· **Accessing evolutionary intelligence** – First, move from the mind to the Living Mind. But there's more to it than just that. Within the Living Mind, you naturally begin to know yourself as a creator. You learn to trust yourself, to trust the abilities and the knowing that comes from this state of living intelligence. It's not just about moving to it and accepting the gifts it has to offer. It's about partnering with the living intelligence to evolve intelligence for us All!

· **Being in the zone** – There is a way of moving into evolutionary intelligence that we call being in the zone. Artists work in this place. Creators work in this space. More than just being aligned, in balance and in flow, it is an awesome experience of connectedness. It is a place of such connectedness to everything and yet such clarity. You don't have to reach for anything; it's right there for you. Every cell of your body is super-connected and alive with amazing, extraordinary energy.

You do not slip up in the zone. You can't. You're so on-line for everything that wants to happen and everything is so crystal clear for you, that you really do know exactly what to do in every single moment. You're in hyper-speed and outside of time and more effective than ever before.

In the zone, you are the holder and creator of all the space, of all the realities. It's a consciousness shift that moves you into a whole new level of creatorship. So ow can you make this shift into the zone? Intend that everything of you is connected to all that is. Intend that all your innate sensory antennae are alert and up for business. Then intend that those antennae connect into the super-mainframe.

2 — Applying evolutionary intelligence to coaching situations

In the energetic dance that is evolutionary coaching, you must reside within evolutionary intelligence in order to create and experience the breakthroughs that are on offer there. From this place, you do whatever is appropriate to do. You dance in the moment, with your knowing fully intact.

Does your client have to be in evolutionary intelligence with you? Not necessarily. You can be there providing guidance, direction and input for them. But it's so much richer if they can move into this same state with you. Then they too can gain their own insights and understanding and you can share the dance with them.

Don't move out of evolutionary intelligence just because they are. No matter where or how your client is operating, the best place for you as a coach is connected to your fullest knowing. It doesn't mean you have to close your eyes and say 'tune in' and all that stuff. It simply means that you operate connected and from there, invite them to do the same, whether it's telepathically, or verbally, or not at all.

Exercise

· **Bandwidth scanning for different interpretations** – In a coaching situation, one of the best uses of evolutionary intelligence is when you can scan the various interpretations of what's happened for them (bandwidth scanning). This allows them to gain insight and understanding of something that might be completely chaotic for them.

· **Tuning into the energy of the communication** – Use your own ability to tune in to translate the energy's communication (e.g. what is the energy of their essence, their passion, their vision). Sometimes your coachee will just see a picture or feel a feeling and not know where to go with that. You can assist with the translation and interpretation to make the journey go smoother and more graciously for them. It doesn't mean that you're providing them with all the answers; they should be looking for themselves as well. Your role is to not to simply tell them and direct them to what you see, but to guide them in following what's right for them. They are responsible for their own journey. You are responsible for providing them with insight and guiding them to their own insights.

3 — Assisting others to move to evolutionary intelligence

The mere knowledge that this kind of intelligence is easily and readily available to us all makes it easier for others to access. So don't hesitate, in the right situations, to have a conversation about it with your clients.

In its most simplistic form, you can coach a client to access evolutionary intelligence by simply taking a quiet moment to relax, breathe, expand, and reflect. Make them aware of the distinction between mind (being in their heads) to find their insights and being connected to the Living Mind to find their insights.

Exercise

· **Tuning in together** – Tune in with your client. Together, seek insights, perspectives, wisdom, and understanding, and then share what you get as a journey of discovery. Keep pointing them to when they're in their heads and inviting them to move beyond that. Get them used to the experience of connecting to the Living Mind and get them on the journey of trusting the messages they receive. The more you and they have trust, the better the information becomes.

· **Intending and pretending** – You could also ask them to intend to move to evolutionary intelligence, and if that fails, have them pretend that they're already there and see how that feels. Pretending something can actually bypass the thinking mind's limita tions and resistance. Or you can ask them what thoughts are in the way of moving to Living Mind. Remember these thoughts will always be cultural and not personal, so be sure to treat them lightly and graciously move them out of the way, so they can have the freedom to experience the delight of evolutionary intelligence and all that if offers.

Engage on the level of potential – Say a client is really frustrated with their job. They can't stand it anymore. How can you as a coach respond? How about with great delight? The client's issues don't have to be the focus. If you focus on the issue as an issue, it's likely they'll shrink and get lost in the sea of seriousness, and before you know it, they're in fear and frustration and everything they touch is wound into that. Instead, use the issues as a vehicle for potential to come on through. As soon as you engage with them on this level, they will immediately brighten up, expand, and move through it with laughter and ease.

EXPERIENTIAL PRACTICE: GETTING IT OUT THERE

· Think about something you've recently had an emotional reaction to. Breathe the energy of it up and run it through the high heart area to place it in the air around you. Then get into relationship with it. See what possibilities it has on offer for you and see what different outcomes this might offer you from the traditional emotional reactive or processing approach. Celebrate it as potential and see what freedom it gifts you.

· The next time you have a client, see where you and they are operating from—intellect and mind or living intelligence and super-connectivity? Where are you coaching them from? Assess where you are and where they are and then dance appropriately.

· Try living in evolutionary intelligence all the time. Notice when you are and when you're not. If you're not, take a moment and simply reconnect to yourself and to the Living Mind. Observe how life occurs from here and explore if you would like to make this a permanent relationship. If yes, go for it by intending it into being.

BREAKTHROUGH

There is so much more available to us as human beings that the evolution of intelligence can give us access to. Life and Creation are waiting for us to do this work, so that as we evolve, All evolves with us. This is what we're born for. It's what we've come to do: evolve Life, evolve Creation, evolve Sourceness. The breakthrough of this chapter is to enable you to coach evolutionary intelligence at will and to bring a new level of evolved intelligence to the whole of the human race.

CHAPTER X
COACHING LEVELS OF POTENTIAL

Intention Of This Chapter
- To open up how we look at human beings and their unlimited possibilities and potential.
- To create a breakthrough in the ease of access of potential.
- To enable coaches to coach the levels of potential effectively, profoundly, and powerfully.

Profound Potential
- To see that we are all mega human beings with a contribution to make; that every single person has mega potential within them and available to them.
- To evolve potential to its next levels.

Key Elements
1 — Exploring possibilities and potential
What's the difference?
2 — Coaching levels of potential
How to surprise and amaze your clients with what they can do and become
3 — Moving from coach to evolutionist
Becoming living potential

Exploratory Discussion
1. What do you think potential is and how do you perceive it?
2. Do you believe that there are levels of yourself that you're not in touch with yet?
3. Have you seen others you've coached break through into new levels of potential? If yes, how did you do that? What was the movement that made that happen?

ESSENTIAL CONTENT

1 — Exploring possibilities and potential

Potential is what can be. Sometimes it's inherent in what already is and sometimes it's brand new, waiting to be birthed into being. Potential is the energy of what wants to happen--with you, through you, and for you, others, humanity and Life. Potential is the well that sources possibilities.

Think of potential as the bigger, vaster, richer ocean from which all things new flow. Possibilities are the streams or pathways that arise when potential rises into conscious awareness. In other words, potential is the ocean from which the rivers and streams of possibility flow. Another way to think about it is that potential is the vision and possibilities are the strategies to achieve it.

Potential is available to happen whether or not you're willing to engage with it. But it does take a conscious intention in order to stir it into being and it does take someone being willing to engage with it to make it come fully alive and real.

Potential requires alchemical movement to bring it into being. You have to do something consciously to realise it, whether it's an energetic breath or a passionate declaration, whether you step into the energy, pour it through into the world, write it, or speak it.

Once potential begins to be realised, then possibilities move into play. You don't necessarily have to do anything to make possibilities emerge; they will pop up for you in the space that the potential creates. But you do need to be consciously aware of choosing the right flow of possibility to bring the desired outcome for the potential. By intuitive feel more than by any kind of logical decision-making, you sense and know the right flow for you.

Exercise

- **Realising the potential in the moment** – Tune in to what wants to happen through you right now. Get in touch with this energy, breathe it on through, get in relationship with it, ask what it is and what it's for. Choose to partner it or not. If you choose to partner it, step into the energy of it and become it walking. How do you feel now?

2 — Coaching different levels of potential

There are three levels of potential:

- Personal (for the individual)
- Greater (for others)
- Evolutionary (for the world, evolution, Life and All)

Personal potential – This is what you're born with. It's within you and fills your energy field. It's all that you can be as you. It's there and waiting to be realised by you and for you.

Greater potential – This is your higher purpose. It's what's waiting to happen with and for others (communities, organisations, nations, and so on). Anyone can access it and work with it. It sits in the air around us waiting to be partnered and brought into being.

Evolutionary potential – This is what wants to be that hasn't ever been before.

Now let us distinguish between *existing creation* (where personal potential and greater potential reside) and *new creation* (where evolutionary potential resides).

Existing creation already exists in consciousness. In the case of personal potential, it's already in your cells and energy field waiting to be. In the case of greater potential, it's in the air around you waiting for someone to pick it up. It has been brought through as a concept before, but may not have been realised, so it's still waiting to be. Personal potential is a part of the already existing path. Evolutionary potential is about creating a new path and becoming Evolutionists for ourselves, others, Life, and all--for the evolution of evolution.

The potential of existing creation tends to be "out there." It already exists in the air around you, waiting for someone to realise it. New creation has never been thought of or called forth before. It's brand new. It is still waiting to be breathed into consciousness. The potential of new creation is sourced from deep within. It is really beyond self, but you access it as a breath from within, and with this breath, you become:

- the source person for it's coming into being,
- the breath of creation, inventing and evolving creation, and
- an alchemist for evolutionary potential.

Let's look at this in comparative format to get a better overview of it:

Paradigm	Potential	For	State	Creation
3D	Personal potential	You & Him/her	What is plus ome steps forward	Existing creation
Middle/Spiritual	Greater potential	You & others	What is waiting to be	Existing creation
Evolutionary	Evolutionary potential	You, others & All	What wants to be newly now	New creation

When you're birthing and realising new creation, you're in a dynamic space. You become more alive. You and the potential are in an evolutionary dance. The joy of it is in the ease with which you dance. In that way, it can actually be more challenging to realise personal potential than to source-create evolutionary potential. When you're in your head (mind), potential is usually not very accessible to you. But when you're in the Living Mind, potential is alive, living, breathing and growing--it is just waiting for you to partner with it. With evolutionary potential you step into a vibrant, dynamic energy that facilitates the alchemical movement.

Traditional coaching works with the client where they are, intending to move them forward toward some level of potential. We are redefining coaches as Potentialists and Evolutionists, where we work with clients as who they really are and all that they can be right here, right now. We don't meet them where they are at--we meet them as they really are!

This is hugely important in evolutionary coaching. It's as if by connecting with and energising that level of themselves that they are pinged into being! You as the witness are like a tuning fork for the wholeness and All-ness of them!

Why would you want to become an Evolutionist evolving evolution? And how does that apply to coaching? When you're coaching another for their personal potential, energetically, it's you and them—that's the total of the energy available to work with. But if you and they step into evolutionary potential, then it's the energy of you, them and All. It now becomes very dynamic, fluid, and engaging. This powerful energy allows you to effortlessly move potential on all the levels, beyond what you can even imagine. The energy of All joins you in the creation of creation.

If you're only coaching personal potential as you and them, then you are holding the space for their next level of potential to be realised. But when you coach evolutionary potential, you open up the space for such enormous breakthroughs to happen that you and they can't even imagine what those might be. You engage with them in a fully conscious choice for living as all they can be. They become the evolutionary potential walking as opposed to just another level of what they already can be. You and they embark on a magically effortless journey of discovery and celebration. It's like falling in love. You see the world in a different way. You're full of openness and hope and everything flows. You come into alignment with all potential and possibility.

From an energetic perspective, you can coach as you and your client are moving the energy OR you can coach within the energy of All that is ready that is ready to move. With evolutionary coaching, it's not about what you or they want, it is about what wants to happen through—and with—you and them.

Can you do this with everyone you coach? It is possible, but it's best done when you and the client agree to play beyond their known selves. It is here that synergy, synchronicity, magica, and miracles move into play. From this place, people will stun and amaze themselves.

It's not about them knowing that they can do it or even having the abilities to do it. Once they step into evolutionary potential, all that they need is available to them. It's a catch-22...a paradox. You only get what you need and become who you need to be, once you step into the energy of it. It's not about getting ready for it or being confident or having learned all the right things. It's simply about saying yes to what wants to be... and then you become it all.

Exercise

- **Stepping into evolutionary potential** – To call evolutionary potential to you, choose to step into it. It's like a breath. You breathe potential into reality and then you choose to partner fully with it. Once you are in the evolutionary paradigm, partnering includes a willingness to invent new beliefs and views around human "beingness" and our abilities and potential. It is only thoughts and beliefs that keep people from moving into greater levels of themselves and we have a lot of old cultural views about what's possible as and for human beings. Imagine a world in which all beliefs were ever evolving in the moment to empower whatever needed to be next and now. To coach evolutionary potential, you need to be willing to evolve even new beliefs with great regularity to have the freedom to invent, create and evolve.

- **Coaching the next level of potential** – If you're coaching someone who can't see beyond their current thoughts and beliefs of themselves and of humanity, have a look at their beliefs and thoughts with them to see which are really true now. Often we're living in old thoughts and beliefs and don't even realise how much we're energetically captured by them. Ask them to say the first thought that comes up for them as they look at taking the next step into becoming who they really are. They will say a thought or belief that will likely be cultural in nature. Once you look at it together in the light of day, it is hardly ever true. Once you've talked that belief over to determine its current "trueness" for them, you'll find that they experience a sense of energetic freedom. The belief has been evolved into something new that empowers them in the now. This is an exercise that you can train yourself to be really aware of and use regularly. From here, sustainability is about learning to evolve our own beliefs in every moment in order to empower ourselves, others and all.

- **Coaching from evolutionary potential** – What if your client actively chooses not to move to their next level of potential right now? Some people may resist your endeavour to realise their and our potential. This could be because they're invested in old or middle paradigm ways and your evolutionary perspective feels threatening to their livelihood and their world view. This is okay. You don't have to move everyone into evolutionary potential and you certainly don't want to judge them if they don't want to go there.

But don't simply buy into their current view of themselves. You can continue to hold the space for their potential and work with them on their thoughts and beliefs to move them towards it. You can also go beyond holding the space to stand in the evolutionary paradigm and coach from there. This is a more co-active and co-creative process. You actually source an active movement with them towards their potential. You move beyond a linear progression of movement within time to an instantaneous possibility of breakthrough and living potential inside the living mind all the time. Your job is to be the catalyst for the living realisation of everything they are and can be, for you and them to become someone different in every moment.

If the client remains committed to no movement at this time, you may want to examine whether you're the right coach for them. You can coach in all the paradigms by your conscious choice, but it is your choice. Some coaches find that their passions exist within only one or two of the paradigms and not all of them.

· **Coaching evolutionary potential**

1. First connect with the person from living intelligence to living intelligence. Next, get in touch with the evolutionary potential that wants to be now.

2. Tune in together to the energy of the evolutionary potential of what wants to happen now and that matches their passions and visions. What is it? What does it mean for them? How does it feel? What does it want? Are they willing to partner it?

3. Bring the energy through and into the air around them. Bring it present and get into a conscious relationship with it. See what it is and gain insight and understanding into it. Then look to see with them if they're willing to step into it. If they say yes, have them make a conscious, energetic movement to step into partnership with the energy. Have them visualise stepping forward into the fullness of the energy and saying YES to it.

4. Ask them how it feels to be walking as this evolutionary potential. Does it surprise and amaze them that they've said yes to this? This is where people discover themselves in ways they have never imagined. You, as their coach, need to support, nurture and empower this breakthrough, ensuring that they are recognised as totally capable of having this potential be realised in the world now. The recognition by you is essential. As it's witnessed, so it and they become

3 — Moving from coach to evolutionist

Working with potential isn't something that you turn on and off, something you put back in the toolkit at the end of the day. It is something you become. There is a moment of surrender when you move beyond working with the evolutionary tools and techniques that live in your mind to operating within the Living Mind as living potential breathing, walking, and talking. You are not just amazed and surprised at yourself and who you're becoming in every moment; you're amazed and surprised at everything you touch, see, smell and work with in every moment.

More than simply accessing or coaching evolutionary potential, what we are talking about is becoming evolutionary potential: Living your life from and for this potential in everything we do. It's about imbuing every moment of our lives with evolutionary potential--preparing food, making the bed, collaborating with people, talking to our kids, and so on. It is at this point everything changes, that we move from being a facilitator for change to being an alchemist for evolution, that we move from coach to evolutionist.

> *Exercise*
>
> · **Living in evolutionary potential** – Look for and see potential everywhere. Begin to relate to problems, issues and pain as potential, because they all are. Remember everything is energy and everything and everybody has potential in every moment. Move into this and see how the quality of the questions and concerns change in your coaching conversations.

EXPERIENTIAL PRACTICE: GETTING IT OUT THERE

· Breathe, relax and expand. Intend to connect to the next level of your own potential. How does it feel? Where does the energy move from and to?

· Using one of your current coaching clients, feel their next level of personal, greater and evolutionary potential. Try out all three levels and notice how you move energetically to access each of the three

BREAKTHROUGH

With evolutionary potential, everything sparkles and comes alive. Big potential and vast vision move from the old paradigm view of massive responsibility to a delightful evolutionary dance facilitated by synergy and synchronicity.

The breakthrough is in who you and the person you are coaching are willing to become in the next millisecond. When we are willing to surprise and amaze ourselves in every moment, we can become living potential realising itself all the time. By sourcing and partnering with evolution we can unfold all we are as a race and all that we can become.

CHAPTER XI
COACHING THE EVOLUTION OF SELF

Intention Of This Chapter
- To understand, access, coach, and experience all the levels of self.
- To live and coach from an expanded megastate and to enable others to access and live it as well.

Profound Potential
- To revolutionise the field of coaching while evolving humankind

Key Elements
1 — The levels of self and beyond
From personality to evolutionist
2 — Coaching who another really is
Calling forth all they can be and recognising it into realisation

Exploratory Discussion
1. When you're coaching your clients, what level of self are you operating from and what level of them are you connecting with?
2. Who are you seeing when you coach someone? What level of the person do you sense you're relating to?
3. Are you willing to be someone new and different now... and now... and now again? See what your intention around this is. Ask your clients this question and see what comes up for them.
4. What's the energetic movement that comes along with setting the intention to continuously evolve yourself and others? Does it feel lighter, clearer with more freedom of movement for you? Or do you feel a panic sense of not knowing who you are and where you're going? If you answer the latter, what is causing you to feel this way?

ESSENTIAL CONTENT

1 — The levels of self and beyond

There are two levels that exist within the framework of the known self: personality and holistic.

The persona or personality self generally orients around the mind, personality traits, and social conditioning. We think we are our thoughts! We tend to see life as something happening to us and not in our charge. Size-wise and energetically, we experience ourselves as a body and a small space of awareness (e.g., two to three feet) around us.

At this level of self, the power is still outside of us and greater than us. As we begin to grow beyond this level, we discover that we're not just a body and that there is a lot more of ourselves to become. We're not necessarily sure what that more is, but it is mysteriously calling us. We seek to know more about ourselves to integrate it into living presence. There's more self-awareness and self discovery.

The holistic self is where you've integrated the greater/higher (spirit) parts of you with the deeper/inner (soul) parts. Once the soul is flipped out and the spirit integrated, then you move completely into a whole new sense of being. You begin to live more responsibly on the energetic and emotional levels. You begin to step into your own power and into the realisation that you--and we--create reality. This is also where you discover living true to yourself, to your passions, and to life. Once you discover this level of self, you actually find it challenging to be untrue in any way.

These two levels of self comprise who you are and who you've always been. It's the nature of you.

The next level is actually beyond self and is a complete recreation of self in every moment. You surrender yourself and discover that from this place you become more than you ever could be. You let go of any concepts of who you are and allow what wants to be to be. You move into an empowering, creative collaboration with Life. Beyond self, self becomes irrelevant, yet in the dance, uniqueness becomes the primary outcome. It's the most magical moment where you truly become all that you and we can be. This level occurs in All-ness, where you know that you are everything that ever was, is, or will be. You become the power of creation.

When you're willing to change, grow, and evolve in every moment, then you're living as an evolutionist. You move into vibrant reality where everything comes alive and everything is possible. You begin to live limitlessly. From this place, the fear of change becomes the signal for the next part of the journey to unfold and for the latest new potential to be realised.

When you tap into something that's totally beyond you, beyond self, life becomes deeply, meaningfully fulfilling. Working with these levels of potential is what really brings life alive for you and for your clients. You and they are mega-changing, evolving the world and more!

You experience, source, and create the movement for yourself, others and all. There is no greater fulfilment on planet Earth than the journey of discovery of all that you and we can be.

Exercise

· **Connecting to the levels of self** —

1. Personality: Feel yourself as a body only and connect to your thinking processes in your head. Believe for the moment that you are just your mind and body. How does that feel? How big are you? Next, breathe, relax, and expand. Allow yourself to begin the journey of expanding discovery.

2. Holistic: Allow yourself to feel really big… as big as your city, country, and even the Earth. From this space, ask yourself, "Am I in mind, living mind, or somewhere else? Is my heart open, my spirit integrated, my soul flipped up and out? How whole do I feel? What does it feel like to be whole?" You'll discover as you move to wholeness that you actively use your heart, your emotional centre, and your senses as parts of your living mind. The holistic you feels in flow and connected; all your senses are activated. But, it's still you and your more holistic mind: brain, heart, spirit and soul.

3. Beyond self: To move beyond self is a simple millisecond expansion from all of you to all-ness. You move from your mind (including all of your senses) to the complete living mind and at that point, it's not just your own senses that are on alert. You have the full sensing capacity of the living intelligence.

2 — Coaching who another really is

Are you coaching to:

- alleviate pain and suffering?
- help clients get past their issues?
- help people improve their lives?
- help them achieve their potential?
- change the world?
- to evolve everything?

These are good questions, but they're not just questions. This is where you come from as a coach. It's the energetic framework within which all of your coaching occurs. By intending to be an evolutionary agent, a potentialiser of potential, you move what wants to be into being. This opens up all possibilities. You open up to all potentials waiting to come on through. You can move what wants to be very easily from this place.

The invitation for you as a coach is to breakthrough from traditional coach to evolutionist, from working with personal or greater potential for others, to calling forth and witnessing the birth and realisation of magnificent evolutionary potential for all. Coaching from and for this level of potential is profoundly fulfilling, for you, for your clients, and for all. You'll also discover that coaching from and for this potential makes things go so much easier and gracious and is a lot of fun!

Exercise

- **Coaching the different levels of self** –

  1. Persona: Think about anyone you're coaching and see them as a body, a personality. Be aware of how you're energetically connected to them. How big are you seeing them and relating to them? How much of their potential can you sense from this space?

  2. Holistic: Expand into your holistic state and then see this same person as who they really are and can be. Meet them whole to whole: your holistic self to their holistic self. What is your energetic connection and how much of their potential can you access and see?

  3. Beyond Self: From the expanded state of all-ness, ask to see MORE and MORE and MORE of them. Relate to them as unlimited potential realising itself. How does this feel? Where are your energetic connections with them now? And most importantly, when you do this with real clients, ask them how they are feeling as they experience these levels of connection with themselves and with you.

- **Coaching someone as all they can be** – Traditional coaching tells us to "meet the client where they're at." Evolutionary coaching says "see the client as they totally and fully can be." Call it forth and recognise it into realisation. It's paradoxical--it won't necessarily happen without your witnessing it, yet all you are doing is asking to see more of who they are and can be. This is where coaching becomes really exciting and you and they move into true breakthrough.

Step way back energetically in order to see them so much bigger and vaster than they actually know themselves in that moment. Now, again, ask for more of them to come present and observe what happens physically and energetically. As you do this, they may have some thoughts, beliefs, or pre-conceptions of self come up that don't allow expansion into these deeper levels. You can either play with the thoughts and beliefs to see if they are really true now or ask them to suspend them for a moment. And as they disperse, more of who they are and who they can be moves into play. This movement often occurs as a whoosh of energy moving to and through them. They'll begin to feel more open, expansive and vital...and so will you.

EXPERIENTIAL PRACTICE: GETTING IT OUT THERE

- Observe the thoughts, beliefs, and pre-conceptions that might be in the way of the clarity and movement beyond self. Yes, it can be scary to take on new things and to let go of the old, if that's what the new is asking you to do.

- Sense where potential is ready and willing to move. Really go for it with everything and everyone in your life. Smell it, taste it, breathe it, see it everywhere. Then once you've gotten in touch with it, move to the expanded state and breathe it into being.

- Move through the levels of yourself (persona / personality, greater / deeper / whole and beyond) to an expanded state of ALL-ness. What do each of these levels feel like for you? In which one do you normally live your life? If you have difficulty experiencing the levels of self, it could be because you may already be living in an expanded state and you have to move backwards to get the other levels. Consider all possibilities as you play with this. For some people, especially those who are energetically aware, this is a natural and wonderful way to be.

- Practice moving clients through the levels of self and potential and see how exciting this kind of coaching can be and how magnificent they really are if you're willing to truly see them as all that they can be. First tune into their personal potential, then greater, then profound and finally evolutionary potential and see how the energy shifts and changes on all the levels. You don't have to go through all four levels in every case, but it is fun to develop this 'potential' muscle and to know where and how you're working with others for their breakthrough potential!

- From the expanded state of all-ness, intend to work for the evolution of ALL and see what happens. How does it feel? Has anything changed? Do you experience movement? Do you feel energy moving to and through you? There's movement that happens when you set your intention. It's just what happens. Suppose you become ALL and find that place of stillness, expanded magnificence and bliss. But if you just stayed there for a long period of time, it's likely that you'd get bored after a while. All wants movement. Life wants to dance. If you truly become all, then you truly want to move and dance and Life and potential moves and dances right along with you.

BREAKTHROUGH

From this place of expanded all-ness, connect with all the coaches all around the world who are willing to evolve coaching into its fullest, newest, mega potential now. What happens? How does that feel? What is the breakthrough of this mega-moment now for us all? Right here, you discover the breakthrough of breakthrough.

CHAPTER XII
COACHING EVOLUTIONARY LIVING

Intention Of This Chapter
- To discover and co-create an evolutionary way of living
- To embody the energy of liveliness and vitality through the dance of life

Profound Potential
- To really claim the individual and collective power of evolution.
- To realise evolutionary living for ALL

Key Elements

1 — What is evolutionary living?
Accepting evolutionary responsibility and partnering with the energy of evolution

2 — Coaching the evolutionary paradigm for others
Bringing the energetic experience of the evolutionary living into sessions

Exploratory Discussion

1. When do you feel energy, vitality, vibrancy, and power? Would you say that's evolutionary living? Why or why not?
2. Do you know when you move in and out of the evolutionary paradigm? How do you recognise this movement and what do you do about it?
3. Do you currently coach evolutionary living with and for others? What happens when you coach people from this place?
4. Can you truly claim that you are the source of —and a force, agent and catalyst for—evolution?

ESSENTIAL CONTENT

1 — What is evolutionary living?

Evolutionary living means:

- Living in the now,
- Creating everything in the moment,
- Being totally alert and aware of potential and possibilities, and
- Operating within a new framework of enhanced abilities.

Once you step into evolutionary living, there's a permanent alchemical alteration to the way you live your life. You experience life differently. You become Life living itself. Evolutionary living and living as and for Life are the same actually.

You live connected to yourself, whole and holistically in relationship with your environment, with others, and with Life.

You live as and for living intelligence and that creates a new set of energetics and an open invitation for new ways of being.

You actually move from one set of frequencies and opportunities to a completely different set of frequencies and possibilities.

Imagine the frequency of life where living is vibrant, fast, juicy, potent, and then compare that to the frequency of life where living is heavier, denser, and slower. One is light and effortless and the other is heavy and burdensomeful. Why is that? Because in the evolutionary paradigm, the energy moves you and you move with the energy. You're not fighting against anything. You're collaboratively co-creating with what wants to be. The energy actually invites you to partner with it.

Look through new eyes at everything and look for potential everywhere. Remember your commitment to the evolution of humanity and the evolution of evolution, or whatever your version of that is in the moment. Make your own full step into the energy of what you're fully committed to. Become it walking!

When movement (change, chaos, challenges, etc.) happens for you in life, relate to it as potential rising. Once you've stuck your hand up and partnered with the evolutionary reality or paradigm, relate to everything that happens as an evolutionary call to movement. It isn't just that you've said yes to another commitment. It's that you've agreed to accept evolutionary responsibility and to partner with the energy of evolution. More than just another thing to do or technique or tool to play with, this acceptance of responsibility and agreement to partner is a Life-realising moment. In fact, it is the Life-realising moment when all that you are and do moves into a whole new paradigm of being. The power here is phenomenal, awesome, and amazing. It's not like the old power at all. It's you and Life dancing for new Life to be birthed and realised. You can't take it lightly, but neither should you feel at all burdened by it. It is profound and delightful.

Sometimes consideration around relationships can have you hold back from taking the leap into the evolutionary paradigm. Some people believe that as they grow and evolve, their partners, friends, and family may not move along with them, and this assumption holds them back from taking the next steps. But it is not true. If you try to hold yourself back for another, in that moment the relationship begins to die.

Instead, be fully you and accept your partner as fully them and all will turn out as it's meant to be. Enjoy the journey of discovery of you and connect with them where you still have strength together. We are not here to be less than we really can be in order to keep others happy where they are.

How can you hold yourself back when Life is being given to you to live more fully, more powerfully, more dynamically, and more creatively? Why would you? We have discovered that when you say yes to evolutionary living, everything turns out better for all involved. When you embrace and step into your magnificent evolutionary power, none of the old hesitations and blocks exist in the same way.

Exercise

· **Sustaining Life in the evolutionary paradigm** – When facing day-to-day challenges, always start from what the world and Life wants from you today. Then, do what's wanted if that feels right to do. You'll discover that Life gets lived a lot more graciously and powerfully.

Become aware when you're shrinking, or have shrunk, in your energy fields and expand. If you discover that you're not in the evolutionary paradigm any longer, move back to it (through the high heart) and revitalise yourself with the energy there. Drink from the well of creative abundance, partner with the energy that is available in vibrant reality.

If you're confused, lost, or distressed about something that's happened to you, move into the Living Intelligence to understand it on a level or levels that you don't yet see. Keep looking for the perspective that will make you go, "A-ha!" That is how you move back into alignment with the evolutionary paradigm.

If you find yourself in a lull between potentials, don't judge yourself where you are.

If you're sick, stop, relax and take care of yourself. Give yourself the opportunity to discover the potential of what's inside those moments. In the evolutionary paradigm, you can heal yourself by seeking the learning opportunities and fulfilment possibilities inside unwellness or disease and then they can magically move away, no longer needed to get your attention for the next step in life. Illness is often your intelligent body's way of saying, "There's something off here and there's something new waiting for you." What if these physical ailments are signals offering the latest opportunities for some of Life's greatest breakthroughs? Our innately intelligent selves actually do know what's up, but sometimes we haven't yet received the message consciously, so the body takes on a partnership role to open you up to this new breakthrough. The more conscious you can get about working with potential, the less you will have unconscious challenges, like illness, offered to you by you. In the conscious state or the evolutionary paradigm, you don't need illness to breakthrough. You can get in front of the wave and ride it like the evolutionary surfer that you are, rather than be dragged by it to the beach.

If you're angry, discover what it is you're so passionate about that's coming up to be realised now. If you're fearful, discover what next steps in leadership are on offer. If it's frustration, have a look at where you're feeling boxed and limited and discover the movement that's awaiting you now. Remember that emotion is really e-motion—energy in motion. Move through it.

If you're feeling low and have no energy at all, find out what's happened to your energy and move it back into flow. It's possible you may have stopped or blocked the energy flow. If that's the case, then consciously discover what's really going on and return to the energetic flow. But if the low or nil energy state continues for any length of time and doesn't respond to reenergising, then consider two alternative options.

1. Ask what's going on in the world and the cosmos that might be affecting you and calling you into a piece of evolutionary work right now.
2. Consider that this might be a complete energy shift—a death and a rebirth, a completion and brand new beginning.

Once you realise you are in a death and rebirth, become your own midwife and allow the birth to come forth as it will. The realisation itself begins to move the energy back into flow.

2 — How do you coach the evolutionary paradigm for others?

You have to be in the evolutionary paradigm yourself in order to offer this shift to those you coach. Both you and the client need to have the energetic experience of it; the power lies in the energy, not in the talking or in the coaching tips and techniques. Talking can facilitate the move into the evolutionary paradigm, but it's the energetic movement that really counts. If there's no movement, there's no shift. Let your commitment to their breakthrough bring you online and into alignment with the evolutionary paradigm.

Exercise

· **Shifting yourself and the client into the evolutionary paradigm during a coaching session** – Work with them on the energy of their passions. That will open the high heart and deliver you straight into the evolutionary paradigm. Try not to care at at all about how it turns out and turn it over to them. Insist they pick up their own power and that they do it for themselves now. This point may seem in opposition to the previous point, but it's not actually. The evolutionary paradigm occurs in paradox, so sometimes dispassionate compassion can actually create the movement for both you and them.

- **Coaching problem solving and goal setting in the evolutionary paradigm** – If a client has a problem, seek to understand the potential within it. See problems as rising potential to be worked with. If you and your client begin working with what wants to happen, all you have to do is stay in the moment for the next right thing to do will become clear.

Goal setting is about breaking down into pieces what you want. But goal setting may not be appropriate in certain circumstances in the evolutionary paradigm. Why? Because the goal you set now may change or evolve in the next few days. Your job as evolutionary coach is to train your client to determine in the moment what's the right next step to do. If you and your clients set goals in the evolutionary paradigm, be willing to let them shift and change them regularly. Partnering with the energy to move something is very different from setting goals to get it to go there. It's not your will. It's your willingness to dance.

- **Coaching through a death and rebirth in the evolutionary paradigm** – Ask, "Is it time for the birth now?" and if it is, go for it. Call the new them into being. Intend it and then reach out in consciousness to connect with the new them that's coming on through. You are the midwife. Coax it, call it, support it, and encourage it. Let this new, precious, beautiful being come in to play in Life with and for us all. These are profound moments and people are radically and magnificently changed by them.

Your client will likely need some quiet time afterwards—as much as three days—to integrate the new energy. They'll want to drink lots of water and stay out of challenging energy places like tubes and shopping malls. They will also want to play with the discovery of the new them. It is really a delight to discover a whole new you!

EXPERIENTIAL PRACTICE: GETTING IT OUT THERE

- Move yourself in and out of the evolutionary paradigm three times now. In – out, in – out, in – out. Explore the energetic movement and strengthen the muscle for that movement.

- Take an issue or problem (yours or a client's) and discover its potential. Once you've done that, how does the energy change? Which paradigm are you now operating in?

- Embody Life if that feels right for you to do right now. Take the step from you and your energy field into the energy field of Life and intend to become it. It's not you walking as Life; it's Life walking as you.

- For the next few days, allow yourself to move with exactly what wants to move through you in any moment without any restriction. Be a potentialist walking. Become the breathing, living, walking, talking reality of evolution evolving itself always.

- Be LIFE walking. Now coach from there and see what happens!

BREAKTHROUGH

Evolutionary coaching is not about helping people get what they say they want. It's about coaching them to bring the next and the next and the next evolutionary piece of work through for them and us all in each and every moment. The breakthrough of this chapter is coaching for evolution!

THE LIVING MIND COURSE WRAP-UP

You have now completed the Living Mind course. It has taken you from the mind inside the head, into a vital, vibrant, creative, dynamic, sparkling, living reality in which you are the source of potential being realised. We've covered passion, vision, clarity, alignment, essence, reinvention, recreation, evolution, possibilities, probabilities, potential and more. Together, we are evolutionising and re-evolutionising coaching and all that it can bring to the world.

Your job now is to live it and to evolve it beyond where we've brought it together. Thank you from all of us for being willing to bring the NEW into being and to evolve LIFE for us all!

COURSE TWO

THE
LIVING
SOUL

CHAPTER I
A ROAD MAP TO WHOLENESS THROUGH THE ALCHEMICAL HEART, THE INTEGRATED SPIRIT, AND THE HOLISTIC SOUL

Intention Of This Chapter
- To provide an understanding and overview of the journey to wholeness.
- To be able to access wholeness from the evolutionary paradigm.

Profound Potential
- To understand, access, and become the grace, effortlessness, elegance, excitement and beauty of living whole.
- To live true to yourself and hand in hand with your own magical essence.

Key Elements

1 — Who are we really?
Redefining the human being

2 — The roadmap to living whole
Journeying into connectedness with All

3 — Movement in the alchemical heart
Evolving the concepts of love and compassion

4 — Integrating the spirit
Expanding your realization of you

5 — The meeting of spirit and soul
Touching wholeness

6 — Evolving your essence
And the essence of All

7 — Living whole
Full alignment and congruence with your true self

Exploratory Discussion
1. What makes up a human being?
2. What does wholeness mean to you?
3. Do you consider yourself whole and / or have you ever felt whole?
4. If yes, what does that feel like? How did you get there?
Can you recapture that wholeness anytime you choose to?
5. How do we become more of who we can become?

ESSENTIAL CONTENT

1 — Who are we really?

Are we small beings on a tiny planet in an insignificant galaxy, helpless with all that passes us by OR are we amazing, profound, majestic beings of wondrous capacity, able to create creation, alter consciousness, and evolve evolution everywhere? Are we tiny specks of little life or are we alchemical Life unfolding?

You can choose which view of life you live in.

We're offering a completely revolutionary shift of perspective on being human and on how to live as new, evolving beings. First we're going to look at the component parts of a human being, as we've been. And then we're going to work with ourselves from a completely new design.

Body – The human body is amazing in its physical complexity and ability. When you consider the physical body as the central focus point for all of you, then it becomes even more exciting. From this perspective, the body is matter *and* more than matter, all interwoven into a holistic experience of self. From here, it becomes the living body, super-connected into All that is.

Heart – The heart is the doorway to expansion and to accessing more of you and All. The heart pumps life force through our bodies... and more. It is a more active agent in the living of our lives than we have ever really known or understood. The alchemical heart is the initiator for evolutionary movement. It's an enabler, not a passive participant, in the journey of Life. It becomes creation breathing itself into being.

Spirit – Spirit is traditionally defined as the higher self and is spoken about as something separate from you, as if you keep yourself from it or it's kept from you in some way. In that model, your power is on the higher planes. But in this course we're going to bring the full extent of your own power back to you in physical presence, as all of you living whole. The integrated spirit reflects all the aspects of you that have ever been, are and will be, rolled up into the wisdom and knowing of the moment. The embodied spirit is you living fully present as All of you. It's the real declaration of I AM. You're not waiting for something to happen. You own your full power and claim your part in creation. With the embodied spirit, all of you is evolving always.

Soul – Soul used to be defined as karmically conditioned and crying out for release. It occurred as something vulnerable and precious that we had to protect from the world by keeping it safely tucked inside. A lot of people haven't allowed themselves access to the living expression of their soul from a fear of it being harmed in some way. But today, soul is dancing into living reality. Our perception of and connectedness with soul is moving from a tiny, protected thing inside us to an all-encompassing, vibrant Life source that gifts us connectedness to everything. We're moving soul from inside us to being all around us and within us. Bringing soul into the living experience of Life is the movement of soul through wholeness to Living Soul. The true power of soul is whole.

Wholeness and essence: Wholeness is where you feel completely and totally aligned with yourself and where the energy of All flows naturally on through you. From wholeness, alignment with self encompasses alignment with essence. Essence is the core of you, the pure source of you. It's where you come from, it's the quality of you that's always there... it's essentially you! From wholeness, essence is more naturally and easily available to you and therefore you can live more true to yourself. It brings essence into your living experience. It's about the clarity, openness and freedom of living as who you really are.

2 — The roadmap to living whole

The roadmap to living whole requires an open heart first and foremost, followed by a connectedness to everything. As you open the heart, the spirit aspects begin to integrate. These aspects include past and future lives, wisdom, consciousnesses, and those parts of you co-existing with you now that you may or may not be aware of. When the heart opens, all of these aspects of you make themselves more available to your conscious awareness. You begin the dance of integrating all these parts of you in the here and now. Does this have to take a long time or encompass multiple processes? It's a personal choice as to how you would like it to happen. It can happen in a flash, it can be a leisurely journey of becoming, or you can resist it and have it be a more lengthy and cumbersome process.

The next step is bringing the soul out to be the receiver for all these aspects or parts of you. How do you do that? You bring your inner authentic self out to play in life. You stand soul naked in the world. You speak truly and you live as who you are--no secrets. You live as transparently you.

Most people have spent their lives finding ways to hide their true self from the world, but the prerequisite for wholeness is a willingness to be open—not vulnerably open but vigorously, passionately, truly, fully, and wholly open. As you open to wholeness, little thought gremlins may arise because some part of you thinks that's keeping you safe. But with the soul out, you discover that true safety comes from living whole, from living aligned and in being true to yourself. From soul comes the true power of whole. From this place, safety doesn't even come into it. You are the source of your own power, living, creating and evolving Life.

In wholeness, your essence is naturally available to you. Connecting with your essence is like an outpouring of you-ness. You're consciously aware of it in every cell of your being. You have a feeling of it. Deliberately focus on your essence and intend for it to be more present with you now. Get into relationship with it. Discover its (i.e., your) qualities. Who are you really? What are you all about and for? We're not talking about life purpose here. We're pointing you to the fundamental source of you. What makes you up and makes you different and unique from all others?

3 — Movement in the alchemical heart

Let's intend to move from an open, somewhat passive heart experience to an active, alchemical heart experience. This means you go beyond the softer aspects of heart, e.g., love, compassion, peace, harmony, which are wonderful to discover and play with. Some people like to experience these softer energies on their journey towards wholeness, to find and unfold themselves along with a new way to be. But once they've experienced and integrated this level, there is often next a desire to move beyond it to something more active and alchemical. The alchemical heart is the combination of the heart and the high heart. This combination creates a heart that's sturdy, strong and an initiator for movement. That's the key difference between an open heart and an alchemical heart: movement!

What often comes up for people making the move from the open heart to the alchemical heart is the question of compassion. Compassion can create a set of energetics that causes both you and the other person to get lost in the trauma and drama. From the alchemical heart, compassion comes from a different perspective; a more detached compassion moves into play.

Detached compassion from an alchemical heart allows for more clarity of movement to actually discover and resolve the issue they're at work on. It's not that you don't care about people, you do. It's that you're focused on what will bring the most movement for them now to take them to their next levels. You don't get caught up in the issue, but instead focus and play with the potential.

What we're talking about is the movement and power of the journey into alchemical creation. It's about transcending how we know love and compassion to be. The alchemical heart is the initiator for this evolutionary movement. With the alchemical heart, we're evolving these concepts and taking love and compassion to whole new energetical levels.

> ### Exercise
>
> · **Moving from the open heart to the alchemical heart** — To open the heart, visualise doors in front of your heart opening onto a garden on a beautiful sunny day. Take a deep breath and breathe in the sunshine. Opening the heart automatically allows nurturing energy states (loving, healing, exploring, discovering, being) to initiate and flow. To open the high heart, think of anything you're passionate about. That opening will allow the sourceful energy (i.e., passion, potential, and power) that facilitates alchemical movement to move through. With the opening of the high heart, the initiation of the alchemical heart can begin. The alchemical heart is actually made up of the heart and the high heart in vigorously open status taken into alchemically active states (transforming, creating, evolving) and working with the energy of potential. Feel as if your heart is a great big magical space in front of you, as opposed to just a small space inside you. Imagine that your heart is an alchemical force in the world and you're its creator. Become this massively great big, magical heart. Remember, it's not passive... it's alchemical. Feel what the alchemical heart feels like.

- **Activating the alchemical heart** – to move from passive to active alchemical mode, make your connection to creation and consciousness from the vigorously open state. Just intend it and see what happens. Now intend to activate your alchemical heart as an initiator, a catalyser for the alchemical states of transformation, creation, and evolution. Through the alchemical heart, the whole of you is connected to creation and creation becomes a natural and gracious state of being. Once the alchemical heart is activated, your connection to your essence and your source energy can be easily made. The inner core expands to allow active, vibrant energy and new power to flow through direct from your source. It's this energy that then facilitates the alchemical dance.

- **Living as the alchemical heart** – The opening of the alchemical heart will create a new life experience; you move from someone living in a reality in which things happen to you to a reality in which you create the things that are happening. When living as and connected through the alchemical heart, the move from mind to Living Mind is gracious and simple. You move from thought to wisdom, knowing and innate sensing as an integral part of your every day, living consciousness.

From the alchemical heart, your relationship to potential shifts and evolves, moving you more towards limitless possibilities and instantaneous reality creation. From here, there's an incredible sense of freedom to be, to create, and to live as you'd want to live. You live the exhilaration of bringing through new things on a consistent basis. You seek change, bring forth transformation, and create evolution. When you're living whole and in touch with your essence, you become essentially you. You can't help but live like this. It seems to automatically come with the territory created by the alchemical heart.

Let your alchemical heart expand to be the heart of ALL. Claim the power of ALL of you ... past, present, future and outside of time.

Now, make magic with your heart. For example, you can love something into being ... but not from a wussy love place, accepting things as they are. More from a passionate, vital, dynamic, sourceful, alchemical love where you're completely in touch with the wholeness of yourself, others and ALL. Witness another into being (see who they really are) and discover the true power of alchemical love, of falling in love with who another really is. This is the alchemical heart in alchemical action.

Think of your most favourite piece of music. Feel it, dance it, love it. Now, realise that even with this wonderful music, there may be potential not yet realised within it. Use your alchemical heart to reach for the purest potential of this music and call it into being. You don't have to know what it is. Simply get your alchemical heart to do its work! Then passionately love the unrealised potential into the music and gift that potential into consciousness for all to receive.

- **Activating the alchemical heart of a client** – Visualise a client in front of you. Become the alchemical heart and intend to evoke a breakthrough for this person now. Just allow the movement and see what happens. Make beautiful, magical Life happen with your alchemical heart.

4 — Integrating the spirit

In traditional spirituality, the embodiment of spirit is more about touching the hem of the garment or about being something so big that's it hard to see how to integrate it. In this course, we're talking about spirit from a holistic perspective, which means that you get to walk around in modern life as all of it, claiming all the wisdom and power of it, translating it into every day speaking and working. It's not about giving your power away to some force greater than you. It's about claiming your own true power.

You have the choice here. You can call to you, and live as any aspect of yourself that you'd like to in any moment. It's only the cultural boxes of expectations of behaviour that might keep you from being it now. So be willing to throw away the boxes and dance in the now. Free yourself to create who you are and to live from a richer and bigger picture understanding. Choose to be amazed at who you really are and how you can really be.

Perhaps we aren't just little people on a tiny planet. Perhaps we carry with us aeons of experiences from many places, beyond time and through many dimensions. What's really fascinating is that when you begin this exploration of other aspects of you, it initially might look like you may be going too far, getting a big head, or leaving the present for some other time or place. But that's not how it turns out. It's the acknowledgement of these parts of all of you that makes the new living of it so very real. The interesting thing is that you don't have to walk around screaming to the rooftops, "I'm a being of light," for example. You can simply walk around expanded, light-filled, and smiling in the knowing that that's who you are. We recommend you let go of the thoughts around arrogance and ego and just play for a bit on a journey of discovery of YOU and see where it leads you.

Some people struggle with self-esteem and lack of confidence. But once you're in touch with the embodied spirit of you, the greater, vaster you, you suddenly discover that self-esteem and confidence are easily available. These aren't qualities that you're either born with or without. They are energetic experiences that are within your control.

As a coach, if you want to work with someone on self-esteem, self- confidence, vision, passion, etc., it's easier if you grow the person (i.e. integrate the spirit and flip the soul out into wholeness), rather than trying to work from the small human being state. With embodied spirit, you have more energy available to you, more presence and more wisdom. All of these come from accessing the expanded energy experience.

There are many ways to access spirit and integrate it. We'll be exploring these throughout this course. The thing to know is that this actually could be a never-ending process of sheer delight as you create an ever newer you. It's not like there's something to become and then once you're there, that's it. You keep growing and evolving, expanding yourself all the time. The spirit journey is simply one part of that expanded realisation of YOU!

Exercise

- **Living as the integrated spirit** — First you have to be willing to acknowledge that there's more to you than meets the eye. You want to acknowledge as real those parts of you that you dream you might be, that you see in meditations and visualisations, those glimpses of past and future glorious you's.

Next you want to be willing to discover, and integrate into your present day living, these aspects of you. So one of the first questions would be 'Are you willing to be the you you've always dreamed you might be?'

You have to be willing to translate who and what you discover you are into modern day terms. You want to find ways to express these aspects of you into living reality. It might be as simple as speaking from an expanded place, bringing new wisdom into what you say and do. It might look like wearing some different clothes that better match your essence or taking a new name for you or for your company that expresses more of who you are.

Be willing to live in this power and create and source Life in the moment as to what's right in every moment. Be willing to be in this expanded space more of the time. Recognise when you're not in this expanded state and step back into it and into your power again.

Suppose you're feeling threatened or emotional about something ... even in the most challenging times, you can call this greater/vaster part of you to you to get you through situations with grace, clarity and ease.

As an integrated spirit, you can choose your own pace of evolution. Karma is non-existent from this place. Destiny is recreated in every moment. Agreements are released and/or remade. This is a completely different and new paradigm. You can choose to live as all you are now. You don't wait to leave this Earth to be all that you are again. In this lifetime, we're about living it all into the here and now, complete with the past and creating a brand new future for us all ... one in which our spirits soar, grow and evolve always.

5 — The meeting of spirit and soul

What happens when soul meets embodied spirit?

It's the feeling of landing, of coming home, of being at one with yourself. It's like the soul is the landing strip for the greater, vaster, deeper, inner parts of you to all come together in one big expanded celebration!

We're not talking about soul in the old ways here. We're not referring to something vulnerable and precious that you hide within. We're talking about the source of your true power, of your essence sparkling into expression into Life. We're talking about living in the strength of the power of Living Soul and the wholeness of all of you connected to all of Life.

The soul is great and powerful and the integrated spirit is vast and enormous. The two coming together gives you a profound knowledge of the vastness and greatness of who you really are. It's the combining of the depth, expansion and profundity of you (soul) with the knowledge, experience and wisdom of you (spirit).

When the soul meets spirit, creation is much more available and possible. We move from static states into creational ways of being. From here, we're more willing to make ourselves up and to co-create new ways that Life can be, as opposed to living how it's always been or how it is now.

Put simply, wholeness is the meeting of spirit and soul. When they meet, wholeness happens automatically. It's like there are no blocks, closures, or holes in the space of you. Your spirit and soul come together into a sense of one big you! You move your energetic state from being connected to the you you've always known (the past) to the you you've always known you really were and are (the future present).

When you move into wholeness, you align the inner (soul) with the outer (spirit) and an alchemical recreation occurs that then allows a complete flow of vibrant energy throughout you, from all directions.

Once you're in wholeness, you live in a new reframe of Life that sustains a vibrant energetic flow. Can the move to wholeness be made in one go? Yes, but it's not always likely or necessary to do it that way. It may take several steps, coaching sessions or breakthroughs to complete this integrated wholeness for a person. If this is the case, simply look to see where their energy is operating at the moment. Is their heart vigorously open? Is their soul flipped out? Is their spirit integrated and embodied?

6 — Evolving your essence

When you're in wholeness, your essence is available to you; it flows up and through you. When you're in touch with essence, when it flows through you, you have access to incredible, true, pure power. Why is that?

1. Because you're super connected to the whole and experiencing what wholeness and connectedness is really all about. You are in that experience as a part of it and all of it at the same time. This is dynamic bliss!
2. Because you're in touch with and aligned to what wants to happen through you at any moment in time and that offers you energetic power surges with a resulting increase in your alchemical input and output.

Essence is the pureness of you, a really clear energy that runs through you and that makes up the very fabric of you. It's the stuff you're made of. It's uniquely your expression of you.

But is your essence changeable? Yes. Everything can be evolved and so can essence.

Is essence uniquely personal? Yes and no. The more you align with the evolutionary paradigm, the more your essence will shift and dance as well. In the evolutionary paradigm, your essence aligns and changes with what's needed for and by All, but it is always unique to you. Your essence at any moment in time can change to match what wants to happen. That means you are not a fixed being. You can enable yourself to shift, change, and evolve always. In fact, you can become the essence of evolution itself or of ALL or of creation.

Essence is the energy of you that comes from the source of you. It's possible that the true source of each and all of us may not have been fully present to us as human beings before now. While your personal essence, as qualities, may have been with you before, your and our collective essence may just now be evolving and becoming more present for us all. As we're willing to evolve our own essence, the essence of ALL can evolve.

Having a changeable essence is an amazing experience of freedom, of flexibility, of encountering, meeting and experiencing different facets of yourself and beyond. You have more vitality as well as a broader knowing of who you are as a never ending, multi-faceted, multi-dimensional being.

Exercise

· **Accessing essence** – simply open up the high heart and the inner core. Connect to the source of you (just intend it and see where and how your energy moves) and then allow the source energy of you to flow on through. As your essence emerges, it might initially be related to qualities and to the movement of energy. But as it continues to reveal itself and as it integrates with the embodied spirit, it can often take archetypal forms via the images that you see and experience. It doesn't mean that you're literally a dragon or an angel, for example. It means that your essence is related to something that a picture or symbol represents more fully than words might be able to express. For example, dragons might represent a fiery connection to creation, while angels might represent a compassionate, healing power.

Explore your essence once it's more present with you. What qualities does it have? How does it feel? If you had to make up an archetypal image to fit this essence, what would it (i.e., you) look like?

· **Connecting to another's essence** – Become the expanded alchemical heart and from that place, enable a profound connection with a person of your choosing. Intend to experience their essence fully, richly, fragrantly, like you're smelling the essence of a magnificent cosmic flower. Be utterly open to being amazed by who this person really is and allow the energetic opening that occurs between you to reveal their essence to you. The essence is a pure thing and it will only come forth in a place of complete respect and honouring.

Notice, as you do this exercise, how you're feeling. How do you feel when you're in touch with the true, pure essence of another? Are you more in touch with yourself... and beyond yourself? Do you have the double experience of being humbled by their cosmic beingness while simultaneously becoming so much more of you? Recognising essence in another creates more essence both in you and in the person you're working with. It's in this space that you can discover evolving essence, because you realise that holding on to who you think you are or who you've always been is actually in the way of your next becoming.

7 — Living whole

Living whole is living expanded and connected to your natural, vibrant energetic flow. It is living fully aligned and congruent with your true self. When you are whole you know when something feels right or wrong to do. You can decide to do it or not do it before you move out of alignment with yourself and out of wholeness.

Living whole is an energetic muscle that we need to learn to exercise. When you're not feeling whole, learn to recognise how that feels and how to move your energy (mind, heart, spirit, soul, essence) into alignment once again.

What can move you out of alignment? Doing something that's not right for you, being untrue to yourself or speaking against what you really believe can put you out of integrity with yourself and pop you out of alignment.

It is possible to be in charge of your energetic state of being. In wholeness, decisions and choices are made more from a sense of knowing as well as a sense of energetic connectedness. Once you've experienced wholeness it becomes more difficult to do these things that move you out of alignment because you feel so much better (clearer, more energised and more whole) when you stay in alignment with yourself. Your antennae are up and if it's wrong for you, your body and energy will signal the problem by indicating the misalignment. Then you simply make the choice to move back into wholeness by realigning your actions with your true intent.

Living whole alters the way you perceive Life, live Life and connect to Life.

Exercise

- **Sustaining the connection to wholeness** – Suppose a challenging situation arises. What do you do? Breathe, relax, expand, and look from a bigger place at what this is all about and for. The understanding of why you've created this situation will restore wholeness to you again. Don't judge yourself or others around this situation. Judgement keeps wholeness at bay.

EXPERIENTIAL PRACTICE: GETTING IT OUT THERE

- Assume that you don't yet know all of you. Assume that there is more to you than meets the eye and that these levels of you are in your consciousness awareness. Make room in yourself for MORE of you to come present into your real life experience of YOU!

- Intend to live whole for a whole day. See how that feels. Notice when you're in wholeness and out of wholeness. What's the difference and are you able to move yourself back into it at will?

- Take the next five clients you have and intend to work with them from and for wholeness and see what difference this makes to the coaching and to the results you achieve together. Observe where they are in terms of their own journey to wholeness ... and remember to stay in the moment with this as they may already be beyond wholeness and into the next levels of evolution. So dance in the moment with your knowing and coach to the level you and they are ready to go to now.

BREAKTHROUGH

Human beings are evolving. We've moved from a closed energy system to an open energy system where wholeness and connectedness to self, others, and All is a simple breath away. The whole of The Evolutionary Institute's work is based on moving you and all of humanity from small, closed-energy beings with problems to solve to vast, open-energy mega beings with contributions to make. That is the power and the breakthrough of living whole.

CHAPTER II
EVOLVING SOUL IN THE EVOLUTIONARY PARADIGM

Intention Of This Chapter
- To understand and to further the evolution of soul in the evolutionary paradigm.
- To discover alchemical grace within the power of Living Soul

Profound Potential
- To consciously become the new Living Soul as part of the evolution of our race
- To consciously co-create that evolution

Key Elements

1 — The evolution of soul
Becoming a living alchemical force sourcing the evolution of Life

2 — Living in Living Soul
We already are

3 — Connecting with others Living Soul to Living Soul
Relating to All as limitless All

4 — Living as Living Soul
Walking, playing, and dancing in the ever-evolving, newest now

5 — The true power of Living Soul
Becoming an amazing mega creator for Life

Exploratory Discussion

1. Are you in touch with your soul? When you are, what does that feel like? Where do you make that connection?

2. Are you aware that soul is evolving? If yes, how are you aware of this and what would you say the difference is?

3. Do you sense the power associated with soul? If yes, how do you access it and experience it?

4. Have you experienced the new quality of alchemical love inside Living Soul? How is that different from love as you've known it?

ESSENTIAL CONTENT

1 — The evolution of soul

In the past, soul was considered to be precious and vulnerable and generally kept inside, safe from the big bad world. Soul was a deeply treasured thing that we learned to keep mostly to ourselves. When connecting with others in soul, the experience was often deeply moving as we discovered a level of pure connectivity. The energetic experience of soul was deeply moving and profoundly stirring. Connecting with others here often felt blissful, calm, restful and profound. But this was soul as it had always been. In recent years, we have consciously begun to evolve the very nature of soul, bringing it passionately, zestfully, creatively and alchemically alive! Hence, the birth of Living Soul.

Today, the new experience of soul is sturdy, vigorous, powerful, active and passionate. Now we live and breathe as Living Soul, actively alive and evolving. We have moved from an old sense of individual self in soul to a growing, evolving, sentiently conscious "soulness" that thrives all around us and within us.

Soul has evolved from an individual experience to a living experience of interconnectedness with everything. The very air is full of this new Living Soul. It's redolent with it. Yes, in the past soul always was about interconnectedness; that is its nature. But now, it is alive with interconnectedness rather than having interconnectedness as its base.

By Living Soul, we don't mean that you live soulfully. That's living in soul and it's a different energetic experience. By Living Soul, we mean that you *become* the new Living Soul and operate as that in all that you do. You make the step from the old paradigm of individuality to the evolutionary paradigm of ultra-conscious, super-connected, vibrant living as an evolving All-ness. In this step the very source of your being and the very source of our collective being is reinvented and evolved. We step into the living experience of reinventing and evolving our race.

As Living Soul, we discover, create and live a vibrant, dynamic interconnectedness with, for and as Life. We become Life and All living and evolving itself. Hence we begin to more actively source Life as Living Soul—as opposed to just experiencing life as a soul.

In Living Soul, Life, All, source, and creation are very interchangeable. It's as if they've all been tumbled into one big, gigantic, alchemical, new being that is sourcing everything everywhere. But this being isn't some distant and far away god that we can never hope to connect with, let alone become. Instead this being is a living alchemical force that is sourcing the evolution of Life as we know it. We have the incredible opportunity of living *as* this new alchemical being and by doing this, we are evolving Life as we dance in every moment. This truly is the reinvention of our race and of the very nature and fabric of being.

Living Soul offers a huge shift in our relationship to new power. Old power was something that you did to another. It was about power over another and could be misused. New power is something that you alchemically breathe and sparkle into being. New power is alchemical super-creation. In Living Soul, you become creation alchemically super-creating itself. You live in accordance with and in a dance with what Life wants. You discover sourcing Life. It's about Life in the grace lanes, dancing with the true power of potential as it bubbles up and offers itself out through you. New power is profound, amazing, delightful, connected and uplifting. It's a feeling of being in exhilarating, collaborative, creative flow and a true experience of dancing with exhilarating creation.

If you recall from the Living Mind course, the access to soul allows the movement to wholeness and beyond. In Living Soul, the access to collective Living Soul allows the movement to something extraordinarily brand new: living fully in the evolutionary paradigm. The step from soul to Living Soul is about moving away from that old reality into a dynamic, vibrant, new, evolving reality.

How does Living Soul connect with and interact with Living Mind? Perhaps they're one and the same, but they can be distinguished and experienced differently. Perhaps the Living Soul is a bigger and more enhanced version of the Living Mind. The Living Mind, as we've related to it in the past, is vast intelligence without beingness. In other words, it mostly occurs like information, knowledge, and wisdom. Living Soul offers beingness to living intelligence. It's where we bring sentient consciousness to intelligence as knowing and wisdom. In other words, in Living Soul everything comes alive. This is where true alchemy comes into play.

Living Mind gives you the understanding of and clarity around what to do to bring transformation, creation, evolution and breakthrough through. Living Soul, dancing with the Living Mind, creates the alchemical power to initiate these movements. When we step into Living Soul we begin changing and evolving the essence of us as a collective and as a race. Living Soul allows for a super-creative process with more power than Living Mind alone seems to provide. Together, they have a catalytic effect on one another and they become something more than just the sum of their parts.

As Living Soul, married with Living mind, we can completely redesign ourselves in every moment. We are alchemical in the very essence of ourselves. We make the move from essence to essencuAllity.

In Living Soul, you have a really strong sense of knowing. Living intelligence is built into Living Soul. You know as if you had always known and it thrills, excites, and amazes you. As Living Soul integrates into every cell of your body, you become living intelligence in every cell of you and the movement from mind to Living Mind changes and evolves. It's less about moving from mind (head focused) to Living Mind (inherently in the air all around you) and more about the evolution of cellular capacity and the evolution of brain capacity to function as All within the physical human body. Wow, We are evolving mind, brain, thought and all of human capacity in this move to Living Soul.

2 — Bringing soul into the experience of Life

Living Soul already exists. It fills the air we breathe and as we create this chapter it's beginning to fill every cell of our bodies as well. All of us already exist within this, but not everyone realises that consciously yet. They may not know how to put it in words, other than to say they're feeling differently.

But do we, as coaches, have any responsibility for opening up the awareness of living in Living Soul? Yes! It's our job as evolutionary coaches to bring that conscious awareness and understanding to light and to Life because the more conscious we are about the way we live our lives, the more powerfully co-creative we all get to become.

As an evolutionary coach, your job is to go with the power of Living Soul and play with it. Speak it, walk it, talk it, and encourage living in Living Soul everywhere. Your job is to coach each of your clients into becoming an opening for magnificent movement and evolutionary shifts to happen. Dancing in new levels of connectivity with the person you're coaching, with Life, with creation and with everything to give you new clarity, focus and fuel. As an evolutionary coach--and as Living Soul--it's about honouring the very breath of Life in order to co-create the evolution of Life.

Become Living Soul walking. What you discover, once you fully become it, is a whole range of new ways to be and to perceive Life. Everything occurs completely different from here. Things become very clear and very much in the moment. It's more vibrant, sparkling, gracious, and creative. Everything is alive and sparkling with Life.

Exercise

- **Moving to Living Soul** — Breathe, relax, expand. Now intend this movement and allow yourself to move into the full, living, rich experience of living soul. Open your eyes, stand up, and walk around as Living Soul. How does that feel?

- **Coaching Living Soul** — If the person you're coaching is already in touch with their soul and has made the step to flipping it from the inner to the outward experience of living it, then moving them to living soul can be easy. From their position of living in and as their own soul and from the wholeness that that creates, now ask them to take the step to Living Soul, the step from the personal sense of soul to a greater, vaster sense of evolving soul for us all.

If the person you're coaching is not fully in touch with their soul yet or if they're having difficulties making this step, there are a number of things you can do to put them in touch with living soul:

- Have them pretend that they are Life living itself. This will get them in touch with the energy of Living Soul.
- Evoke the movement to Living Soul through your living language. When you become Living Soul, you speak it as well. You're alchemically speaking for the movement of energy, so if you allow yourself to do this, then the movement for the person you're coaching to Living Soul will be evoked.
- Alchemically power-love them into it. This is about understanding and igniting their deepest and vastest being by getting who they really are. Witness this being into becoming and recognise that in Living Soul it is not an individual becoming; it's a collective, interactive dance of becoming for All.
- Hold the reality that they already are in Living Soul and whenever that realisation is right for them to have, they will naturally and automatically become it. In

> fact, if you operate from the certainty that they already are that, then it makes the job gracious and simple.
> · Let them know that they are already it. Explain the journey of soul to Living Soul in whatever way works for you and for them in the moment. Help them to understand what it is they've been going through, but didn't have language for before. You don't have to use our language and interpretation of Living Soul to explain it to another. Let Living Soul speak as you--as your unique experience--and share whatever brilliant perspective lights up Life from that sharing.

3 — Connecting with others Living Soul to Living Soul

Connecting in Living Soul is a fluid, multi-faceted experience, as opposed to the linear experience when one person connects with another. Everything is fluidly dancing and interweaving. The connection happens simultaneously with all the levels. We delightfully connect with the magnificence and beauty of others from Living Soul.

If you know without a shadow of a doubt that we're all already there, then it is already so. We're already vibrantly inter-connected. From here, we discover that whatever wants to be spoken or coached in the moment dances into being.

Human connectedness in old soulness left us feeling separate, at the far end of the scale and deeply touched by another at the other end of the scale. But being connected in Living Soul is a vibrant and sometimes ecstatic experience rich with delight, recognition, and a glorious acknowledgement of the magnificence of us all. In Living Soul, when any one connects to any other, the whole is shimmered alive. It's an alchemical invocation of our evolution with every breath.

In Living Soul, you're automatically with another as more than just the physical, more than just their higher energy, more than just their soul energy. You are with them like they're everything and you're everything too. But you don't necessarily experience this as oneness. It's more like being uniquely the whole relating to another who's uniquely the whole.

This new movement of connectivity occurs very fluidly because in Living Soul we don't tend to have thoughts or beliefs around what it is to be human. There's a more fluid openness to who we are and who we can be. You can be with another limitlessly, without frameworks, perceptions or assumptions. You allow for that which wants to become, whatever that is. Anything can happen here. You can actually be working for the evolution of the race as you coach, dance, and simply be.

How do you connect with others collectively in Living Soul? Intend it and you will discover an initiation of connections all around you. You will become the whole super-connected as one vast living presence. Again, it isn't quite the same as being one. Oneness is often a peaceful, contented, even passive experience. But in this new Living Soul collective-all experience, there's a delightful, vibrant, omnipresent experience of your own uniqueness along with everyone else's.

Inside this experience, you may discover that the abilities of each and every one are on offer for the whole. Let this sink in for a moment. Perhaps our gifts and abilities are no longer uniquely built into our souls and essence, but instead are a full array of gifts and abilities on offer for everyone to select from. In Living Soul, therefore, anyone can be a genius, anyone can be an artist, and anyone can be a leader. It's all available and on offer for All.

In Living Soul, vibrant openness and truthfulness are present. In Living Soul, we learn to be open and transparent. What's to hide when we're all so interconnected and sourced from as well as sourcing the next newest levels of ourselves? In Living Soul, we discover a willingness to reveal ourselves in our totality in order to bring it all into living presence. On some level of ourselves, we are already the evolving being of our new race. It exists in consciousness, even though it is just newly, recently created.

As a coach, you can facilitate the movement of our conscious evolution by supporting the people you coach in bringing this knowing and evolving more into living reality. You can partner with them in the evolutionary dance. As a coach, you can evolve the human race with each and every session. You can unfold our limitless possibility with every breath. If you're truly aligned with this knowing, everything and anything is possible.

How do you stand in the knowing that the people you coach already are this evolving being, while the process of their becoming is still unfolding? You align and connect yourself with that level of their being and know that as the living reality. Then you interact with them from there. You don't have to be in their dream of what is real or not real. You can align with the evolving version of this magnificent, extraordinary being. As a coach, you want to stay true to that no matter what the current reality or their perspective of their living experience is. If you can continue to engage with them from here, their experience of living it becomes easier and easier.

In order to do this, there is a bigger picture at work here. You have to be willing to allow humanity to evolve as you coach each and every person. In other words, you have to be the Living Soul of us all evolving itself through this journey of connectedness and becoming. Be willing to know all of your client's purposes, passions, and visions to be so much more than anyone has ever even imagined before. Put no limitations on their possibilities. As you coach their passions and visions into reality, discover yourself as an Evolutionary Wayshower who's creating leaderful players on the evolutionary team.

Is it right to be with someone or even all of humanity on this level if you or they think they're not ready for it? Yes, because the world is a better place for it. Sometimes the difference between where you see them and where they are might be huge, but if you ask them to just allow it instead of trying to figure it out, everything moves with ease and grace. Allowing it to be so creates an amazing dance of unfolding, gracious becoming.

Exercise

- **Connecting Living Soul to Living Soul** — Intend to connect with someone that you know and love as Living Soul to Living Soul. Visualise that person in front of you and then open to the possibility that you haven't got a clue who they really are and can be. Vigorously open and intend to discover their evolutionary contribution to us all. What happens when you do that? Try relating to them as if you are AllLand they are All and enter into the alchemical dance of possibility with them, as limitless All to limitless All.

· **Collective connecting as Living Soul** — Be the Living Soul and know, sense, feel, and connect with the living tendrils of the interconnectivity of everything. By just intending it, you'll experience yourself becoming more. Be willing to go beyond your own known perceptions of yourself and dance in the experience of the whole.

4 — Living as Living Soul

Inside Living Soul, you are also in Living Mind, alchemical heart, integrated spirit, and so on. In truth, these aren't separate things; they are distinguishable only to allow you to create alchemical movement. It's a dance of subtle nuances and movements within a living space of ultra-interconnectedness that creates the whole evolutionary paradigm.

Intend to walk as Living Soul and see what happens. Allow yourself to become it and set your intention to live as that for however long you wish. You can make this a permanent shift, but always be willing to allow yourself to evolve into whatever is next. Right now Living Soul might be the thing, but tomorrow it might all shift, dance, and evolve to the next levels. You have to be willing to keep moving, becoming, and evolving. That's the wonderful thing about the evolutionary paradigm... it never stands still and we are the ones that are creating and stewarding that movement.

Expand into the fabric of Living Soul. Be willing to experience it, express it, laugh it, dance it and sing it. Don't just sit there waiting for something to happen. You can alchemise it through your intention and the energetic movement that intention creates. Believe that it is possible and know that you can do it. Throw away any old thoughts that say this is silly or impossible, and dive into the energetic experience.

If you observe young children, they're already there. This state of being and becoming is actually natural to us. Step into the playful interaction of being in the moment and dance! If you find yourself out of the now, move yourself into the present and from here into the ever-evolving, newest now.

Be willing to be Life evolving itself. Try this on and see how it feels. If it isn't quite how you see yourself yet, try it on like a set of clothes and see what feels right for you. Play with it till you have the perfect fit!

Exercise

· **Living as Living Soul** — Pretend to be a kid who is already living, walking, playing as Living Soul. Don't choose a particular child, just intend it more generally and allow

> the energy to guide you to the right experience. Ask yourself if you're already living as Living Soul and/or if this has already evolved into something new for you. Trust your evolutionary sensing to do what's right for you in the moment. If you've just taken on living as Living Soul, how does that feel? How is the experience different from your normal experience of life? You can come in and out of the experience of living as Living Soul if you wish to, but you can also intend to become it fully, if that feels right to do.

5 — The true power of Living Soul

The true power of Living Soul is that it's limitless. Anything is possible. There are no frameworks here. You throw away all of the old perceptions and boxes of how things are and you dance very much in the moment of the magical becoming. It's always in magnificent flow. Where the true power of soul is whole, the true power of Living Soul is creatorship. It's hugely creational fun.

In the true power of Living Soul, you have a feeling of real interconnectivity. Everything is available to you there. You're interconnected to everything and you realise that you are the creator of reality. Once you accept the true power of this, you become an amazing mega creator for Life! Along with this comes the responsibility—your ability to respond and naturally, playfully, move things into being.

The true power of Living Soul is new power, a creational, alchemical power that dances with Life for evolving newness, for the evolution of love, grace and Life in Living Soul.

Love and grace in the old paradigm have a certain energetic sense to them. They're lovely, but mostly without movement attached to them. In the old paradigm, people were looking for love as something to fill a hole in them.

In the evolutionary paradigm, as an expression of Living Soul, love and grace are ever-evolving, increasingly powerful forces of and for creation. They become more dynamic, active, and alchemical. Evolutionary love and grace are dynamically infused through everything. They're part of the fabric of Living Soul—active ingredients and catalytic converters for pure potential to be realised. Love and grace then become much more alchemical than we've traditionally known them to be.

You have to be willing to completely redefine love as you know it. It's way beyond anything we know of love and it's definitely not unconditional love, which is allowing and nurturing in nature, but NOT alchemical. Alchemical love and grace is so active that it almost begs new words. In the evolutionary paradigm, alchemical love initiates the holistic, ecstatic, ultra-connected experience of Life! You're in love with the very essence of Life itself and in the loving of it, Life is evolved. It's a sparkling, shimmering movement, not clinging, needy or demanding.

Step into the dynamic movement of alchemical love and allow it to carry you purposefully and energetically. Experience the fullness of this movement. You'll discover as you move this new alchemical love into play, that grace automatically flows with it. It's a new kind of love and a new kind of grace that has an ability to free flow, to evolve itself, to become more than it's ever been. In the evolutionary paradigm, you evolve love and grace as you move and dance!

> *Exercise*
>
> · **Mega-creating in Living Soul** — Breathe whatever the next pure potential is through you as All evolving All. It's a whole body and being breath, not just a wisp of a breath through your chest, throat, and mouth. Breathe with your whole being and call forth from whatever wants to be through you now. Walk, live, and play in this alchemical power. Do things that you might not have dreamt you ever could do. You are the power of Living Soul, moved from a small being with limitations to an all-powerful and all-knowing being. You are the new power source for Life. You are Life walking and you fall madly, wildly in love with Life all around you.

EXPERIENTIAL PRACTICE: GETTING IT OUT THERE

· Walk around for a full day conscious of living as Living Soul. Notice what's different about this experience. Is this something you would choose to live as all the time? If yes, go for it. You know what to do! If not, play with the thoughts that shape that choice. Are they really true?

· Begin working as Living Soul with at least one of your clients and see what kind of results you can achieve from this level of interconnectivity and alchemical power. Be willing to breathe their pure potential into the dance, into the spaces between you. Offer it out energetically to them in that dance in whatever way feels right to do.

BREAKTHROUGH

Be curious. Be willing to be surprised. Prepare to be amazed! Human beings are becoming something we have no precedent for. From here, the possibilities for our evolution are limitless. The breakthrough of this chapter is discovering the limitless power of living as Living Soul. The breakthrough is in engaging with the evolution of evolution, the potentialising of potential, in becoming the active ingredient for, and the initiator of alchemical movement.

CHAPTER III
PROFOUND POTENTIAL –
COACHING THE BRILLIANCE AND
POWER OF INNATE BEING

Intention Of This Chapter
- To discover the evolving differences between essence in soul and essentiALLity as Living Soul and Living Source Soul.
- To learn how to coach an evolving innate being, empowering others to access their unique brilliance and give it full expression in Life.
- To be able to call forth brilliance in everyone.

Profound Potential
- To weave innate brilliance into the evolution of the human race.

Key Elements
1 — Discovering essential uniqueness (in soul)
Honoring all that you are
1 — Discovering essential uniqueness as ALL (in Living Soul)
Profound super-connectivity that evolves beingness
1 — From essence and essentiALLity
Getting in touch with our collective innate brilliance
1 — From Living Soul to Living Source Soul
Becoming the conscious evolvers of beingness and therefore of our vibrant reality

Exploratory Discussion
1. Are we what we're born as or are we ever-evolving beings?
2. How do you honour your essential uniqueness?
3. Where do you find innate brilliance and essential uniqueness in yourself and in others?
4. Are you willing to be complete with who you are in order to step beyond yourself and into Life and All?
5. What is the living expression of your essentiALLity?

ESSENTIAL CONTENT

1 — Discovering essential uniqueness (in soul)

Every person has extraordinary uniqueness in them. It's what makes humans so precious as a race, yet our cultures haven't found a way to honour this completely yet. Consider how the education systems in our western culture are based on adherence to a norm--the opposite of honoring our miraculous uniqueness.

Much of the angst in Life is about not measuring up or not fitting in. But what if you could coach from a completely different orientation? What if instead of getting your clients to align with what they perceive they're aiming for, you offer them the extraordinary magnificence of becoming all that they can truly be?

What if the quest for being and becoming is based not on a standard of normality, but on a complete and utter seeking, honoring, and expression of our essential uniqueness? This isn't just a concept, by the way, it's a whole new way of perceiving and living Life in the evolutionary paradigm.

How do you discover this magnificent uniqueness in yourself and others? The answer lies in Living Soul.

Each soul has always contained a unique patterning of source. It is the blueprint of YOU. But in the past, we've perceived that uniqueness as fixed. In other words this is your soul, these are your qualities, this is who you are, and how much you can be. In Living Soul, this blueprint is freed from just one way to be and becomes a creatable and evolvable essence.

Essence is the aspect of soul that you uniquely represent. In soul, you simply reach inside to feel your essence at the core of you. It has always been there, cohesively and consistently over time. But in Living Soul, essence pops through newly in every cell, as if you are Life evolving itself into something brand new in every moment. You are in the creational discovery of a brand new essence of yourself in every moment. Before, who you were was who you were. But now, in Living Soul, you are recreating yourself in every moment from the pool of everything and every creation that you make of yourself is your uniquely evolving essentiALLity.

essentiALLity liberates the creation and evolution of ALL-ness and from here, every human being is essentiALLy redesigned. The Life power in this is wonderful. It's not about forcing things or demanding to be something different than we are. It's about dipping into the pool and the power of Life, into the vast oceans of All to pull out any kind of being you choose to become.

But before we dive into evolving essentiALLity, let's look first at connecting with your essence as it's always been.

Exercise

- **Living as your essence** — Your essence has always been who you are and your blueprint is more of a plan of how to express and live that essence into its fullest possibility. You can be uniquely you regardless of what's going on around you *and* you can live fully into your blueprint.

Feel into the core of you and allow your essence to come to the fore. Revel in and discover the blueprint of your own essential uniqueness. What are you discovering about yourself? From this essence, be willing to call forth all of you. Be willing to step into and become the essence of you full-on present in the now. How does that feel?

Make a conscious choice to live your essential uniqueness. When you go into environments where you're not being seen, heard or known, it's easy for your energy to slip away or pull in. Remember to open up and expand, bringing more and more of you into the present.

Straighten up, take a deep, full body breath, and expand your inner core, so there's more room for the essence of you to be present.

Be willing to let go of how the world sees you and learn to live true to you and who you really are. Don't buy into others' views of you. Instead play with, discover and learn to live as full-on you. Revel in you and dance with your essence. The more you live your essence, the sturdier and stronger your essence becomes, the more it allows itself to be seen, known, and heard by the world because as who you are.

- **Coaching someone to discover their unique essence** – Ask where they feel their essence. Allow them to discover where in their body it resides and then engage them in bringing the energy more present.

Once the energy of their essence is present, have them get into conscious communication with it to discover its qualities and texture. One way to do this is to have them place the energy of their essence in front of them and talk to and feel into it.

What makes them different from all others? What makes them unique? Engage in a conversation with them around their uniqueness and in the process, their essence will reveal itself and come more present for them.

Another way to do this is to pretend to be this person and breathe their essence as if you were them. Discover the qualities and feel of who they really are and feed it back to them. This will help them to be more consciously in touch with the energy of their essence.

2 — Discovering essential uniqueness in Living Soul

There was a time when accessing the fullness of your uniqueness was an awesome accomplishment. Today, we hold the possibility of moving into so much more. In Living Soul and in ALL, the essence of you is freed from being eternally fixed. We are fluid beings with the possibility of accessing an ever-changing becoming.

How is the essential uniqueness of you and the essential uniqueness of you in All different? When you're in Living Soul--in evolving All--you hold the keys to a limitless experience of possibility. In the past, we were blueprinted in an individualistic and closed energy design. But today, we are discovering our evolving blueprint for ourselves as individuals and as a race.

From our new open energy system, we can reach into All and select the next level of evolving being that we each desire to become. We can also call forth the next level of being for our collective co-creation. The essential uniqueness of ALL is ever evolving and ever re-creating itself. Now that we have finally gotten into relationship with our evolving essence we are redesigning ourselves accordingly.

Discovering the essential uniqueness of you has been a journey of discovering what you're already capable of. Discovering the essential uniqueness of you in Living Soul is a creational process, ever unfolding and re-creating.

When you step into Living Soul—into the vast, sentient, conscious presence of everything, of All, of Life evolving itself—you step into the full power of our new levels of connectivity. In soul, we were essentially connected, but not necessarily very aware of that connection on the physical plane. In Living Soul, we are living new levels of ultra-connectivity.

The move from soul to Living Soul is like stepping from you as an individual, all alone and just you, to you as All, super connected and vibrantly, consciously living as All. We thrive in this fuller, richer presence of All that surrounds us and is us. Perhaps most simply said it's a profound connectivity to Life as Life. It's where the power of All meets Life! It's an act of profound connectivity that alchemically creates new becoming. In Living Soul, you become source sourcing sourceness, creating creation, and evolving evolution. You become responsible for the design of you and for the design of beingness.

From here the next step is to own this evolving beingness. Instead of moving in and out of this state of being and becoming, you can choose to be the fluid, dynamic, living expression of Life and All always.

Exercise

- **Moving to Living Soul** – Breathe, relax, expand. Now intend this movement and allow yourself to move into the full, living, rich experience of living soul. Open your eyes, stand up, and walk around as Living Soul. How does that feel?

3 — From essence to essentiALLity

Essence is relating to who you are and what you're all about from a personal place. essentiALLity is relating to who you are and what you're all about from the evolving All. It's a complete shift of being. It's not just about perspective and how you see yourself and the world. It's the place from which you orient yourself.

Essence and essentiALLity are different energy sources of your being. If you're in essence, you're sourcing from your own energy or from original soul and source. If you're in essentiALLity, you're sourcing from a new energetic Life source that we're calling Living Soul. When you become this source energy walking, you are sourcing new Life into being. The difference between essence and essentiALLity is also related to power. In essence, power can come through you and you're an instrument of that power. In essentiALLity, you are that power. You source it into being.

Once you've made the move from your personal essence to new essentiALLity, the next step is to own it, source it and live it. Creation and consciousness become a living part of you, no longer separate from you.

When you move from soul to Living Soul, from essence to essentiALLity, and from old paradigm reality to new paradigm, everything comes more alive and is more enchanting. You engage with Life differently and you have a different experience of daily living and of yourself. You are different. You become a consciously creatable, evolvable being.

Innate brilliance is the shining ability to fully express all that you are. Has innate brilliance always existed? Probably, through brilliant artists and the relatively few creative geniuses we've seen here on Earth over time. In the move to Living Soul, however, innate brilliance becomes accessible to any and all. It may also be newly evolving, built in to the redesign and evolution of humanity and of beingness. When you allow yourself to be uniquely and essentiAlly you, you are fully expressing your innate brilliance.

Charismatic presence emerges when you are the expression of your unique essentiALLity and when you're in touch with your individual and our collective innate brilliance. This is where true charisma comes from and where new leadership really sources into being. True charisma is about being such a full-on expression of Life and Self, along with ultra-connectedness with others, that people are called to dance with you. Charismatic leaders are really essentiALL people, connected with an amazing brilliance that is far beyond themselves as individuals. With Living Soul, this charismatic presence is now more readily accessible by everyone. From this state of being, all of Life comes along with you for the dance. It's fun, delightful and gracious. It's also zany and creative as well empowering and inspiring.

The step into essentiALLity, and therefore into charismatic living and leadership, is a new energetic movement. From head, mind, and old soulness, we normally connected from inside out, leaving us feeling distinctly separate from others and Life. As we initially step into Living Mind, the movement of the energy is again from inside out. We move from the mind to the Living Mind around us. But as we make the shift to Living Soul and its integration with Living Mind, we begin to become and integrate with Life and All that is outside and around us. Every cell is activated to come alive sentiently conscious and completely capable of sourcing sourceness, creating creation, evolving evolution. It's as if consciousness and creation move into the living experience of every cell. We are becoming a brand new beingness.

As we step into Living Soul, our cellular antennae connect physically to everything. Every cell begins to feel more alert and alive and connected to everything on every level. This is the process as we write this chapter, so it may change over time as it integrates more fully into the human evolution.

4 — From Living Soul to Living Source Soul

Recently there's been a definitive move from life force—traditional energy sources like the sun, nutrition, and so on— to Life Source, a new, vibrant energy source that's pulsing through the air and also generating from within in partnership with our new cellular structure. Actually, what's happening here is a step from Living Soul to Living Source Soul. Living Soul allows us to live interconnected with Life and All. Living Source Soul provides us with the possibility of living uniquely *as* All, as source, as an incredibly inspiring and empowering way to be. Another way to say this is that through Living Source Soul, you become Life alchemically evolving itself.

Your essentiALLity is your unique expression of this newly, evolving sourceness. There's vitality in your presence because you are sourcing vitAllity and are manifesting the new essence of All. Your energy expands even more, but you don't overwhelm, overpower, or over-do it. This presence is different than we've experienced before because it sources from connectivity. It's sustainable, sturdy, and vigorous, but also offers the space for others' presence to be manifested.

This kind of presence doesn't take up all the space or impose upon others. It does the exact opposite. It creates the space for presencing and invites others to join the dance, to come fully into their own essentiALLity and presence to play in the full expression of their uniqueness. The more each person expresses this presence, the more everyone gets to become it. This energy enables and creates the space for others to become.

In the past, charismatic leaders often took up all the space. In other words, they were the focus of the movement. With essentiALLity and this new energetic Life Source, you can be charismatic and innately brilliant while creating the space for everyone to naturally and uniquely become charismatically leaderful as well. It's the move from leadership as an individual thing to leaderful as a collaborative dance.

This movement from essence to essentiALLity, from soul to Living Soul to Living Source Soul, integrates the step beyond self into All and weaves it back into your physical presence in a brand new mega way. Moving into essentiALLity as Living Source Soul happens in a movement of completion with all that you are and have been. You fully integrate yourself on all the levels. You're complete with yourself. It's inclusion, acceptance and fulfilment, not letting go or surrendering. It's a full becoming. It's a coming together of all the levels of self into one magicAll moment. You move into a whole new level of being, an evolving being capable of evolving everything. And it's here in this magical step that the reinvention of our race truly begins.

We are becoming source walking, creating and evolving itself. In other words, the dwindling life force energy that we used to live on as carbon-based beings is now Life Source energy that sources Life as crystalline-based beings. Although we don't have scientific evidence for that yet, we do have the collated experiences of many people co-creating, feeling and living this shift. Living as new sourceness is like plugging into a new energy source that's free flowing and everywhere. You then become this energy source to sparkle, emanate and infuse it into Life. This is experiential, so don't try to think about it too much. Just move to Living Mind and iving Soul and allow it to just happen.

Why would someone want to connect with and become this new sourceness? It gives us vitality and access to vibrant power, which offers us the sourceful, creative, collaborative and connective power upon which the future of our emerging world is being built. From here, we discover new levels of creative genius and reality creation. We become the conscious evolvers of beingness and therefore of our reality.

As we become this new sourceness, and express it through our unique essentiALLity, we naturally begin to exist in and co-create a vibrant, new reality. When coaching others in the evolutionary paradigm, it's essential to move them into vibrant reality. Once anyone opens to and moves into this vibrant new reality, they are automatically in touch with vibrant, new source energy. It is this energetic shift that will source hugely creative and evolutionary shifts easily and graciously within them and through them.

To access the full power of innate brilliance and being, you must fully express your evolving essentiALLity. Be willing to be complete with who you are in order to step beyond yourself and discover a whole lot more that you and we are all capable of now. Remember this is about reinvention and evolution.

Can we complete, fulfill, and become all we are now? Is this possible? It is.

You don't have to seek for answers. Instead simply move into the knowing of the Living Mind.

You don't have to get relationships right. Instead move into ultra-connectivity of the Living Soul.

You don't have to learn how to wield power. Instead become Living Source Soul, become All and discover the in-the-moment dance of vibrant, alchemicALL power. This is where the real journey of our conscious evolution begins.

It's more than just completing with the persona self. You're completing with the essence self, which includes the persona self, the higher or greater self, and the soul self. You're completing you as you have known yourself to be. It's not a death or rebirth. It's a simple choice. Then, you choose to step beyond your essence self into your evolving essentiALL self with grace and ease.

As you move into your essentiALL self, you can choose to be anything you want to be. It's fully creational. So if you want to keep any or all of your essence as it has been, you can do that. It's equally possible to move completely into your evolving, essentiALL self and let go of the old essence self completely. Whatever you wish to create is brilliant and fine.

Can you radically revolutionise your essence or is your essence always your fundamental essence? Do you want to hold on to any way of being that you feel is especially you or can you evolve in every moment for what wants to be, with absolute freedom and liberation?

The answer is whatever you choose.

Perhaps the true, powerful, innate brilliance and being occurs beyond self. This is about the evolution of self, so that the self integrates with the beyond self, and the All self pops on through to become your living experience and expression of Life. You become All and Life walking, evolving beingness as you do so.

Evolving beingness is a brand new way to be. It's about the full presence of source power. This is the reinvention of our race, exciting, ever evolving beings who are profoundly present to the power of the moment. To coach someone into newly evolving beingness:

> From this new source energy, innate being is an ever evolving, creational experience of becoming. We're not fixed human beings, we're mega beings evolving beingness. Everything is available to us to create in every moment. Who you've been in the past is irrelevant to the present moment. It's not about letting go so much as simply becoming. In the

old reality, people generally have had difficulty in letting go of the past or of who they think they are. But in vibrant reality, letting go is no longer relevant because you're in the evolvable moment and you create. Being willing to continually become creates the movement that sets our conscious evolution into play.

To coach and evoke others into the brilliance and power of innate being, you need to be it yourself. As you become it and be it, so others are evoked into it through your presence, through the living expression of your essentiALLity. It comes through the reverberation of your voice, the alchemy of what your eyes are willing to see and the deliciousness of what your senses are willing to create. You become the evoker and creator of reality, including the evocation of it in others. This is a natural occurrence and there is no forcing it against someone's will or free choice. You simply become the vibrant reality of new source and invite them into the dance. In truth it's already there for everyone and perhaps this is how human beings were always meant to be: connected to Life, to source, to All and living in the garden of creation.

Exercise

- **Coaching the newly evolving beingness** – Have them connect with and feel their soul's presence. Just ask them to do this and see what happens. It's not the movement here that matters; it's their access to the quality of the energy of soul and essence. Once their soul is present, have them get in touch with their essence and describe it in terms of quality of energy and how it makes them unique. Encourage them to step fully into the energy of their essence and to become it. They may now need some time (from a few minutes to a few months) to integrate before you ask them to be complete with this step and move to the next level. You don't want to slow down or limit the experience, but at the same time use your knowing of what's right in the moment for each person. You and they will know when the time is right to step beyond essence into essentiALLity.

When the time is right, there will be a sense of completeness with self. You can work this through with them to completion, but often when the time is right, completion seems to naturally occur. To work with them through to completion, ask the question "Are you complete with you now?" That doesn't mean they're going to leave the planet or anything like that. What you're really asking is, "Are you ready and willing to evolve yourself beyond anything you've known yourself as before now?" In conversation, you can get them to the place of saying yes to these questions and being ready to evolve. Once they're ready, they're poised on the cusp of their and our conscious evolution.

Next is the step from soul to Living Soul. Have them expand their energy and get in touch with the living presence of source, All, creation, and consciousness that surrounds us now. From here, have them visualise the antennae of every cell connecting in with this presence, so that they're fully, ultra-connected and can begin to get the sense of becoming All.

Ask them to connect with their essentiALLity, their mega uniqueness, in the presence of Living Soul. Getting in touch with essence tends to be more focused on a specific energetic source. But getting in touch with essentiALLity is more expansive and allows them to dip into the pool of evolving source to discover and create their evolving essentiALLity from a brand, new source energy. Each person may do this differently, so ask them to intend it, do it, and then see what happens for them. If we prescribe this journey too succinctly, we might actually get in the way of the creation in the moment.

The key here is to explore and unfurl new sourceness. This began as a place inside of us as we remade our connections from soul to living soul. The connection may have been different for each individual, but generally we were co-creating new sourceness with this move. Consider it like this...what if the energy and the space in which we live and source ourselves from has evolved in just the last few years? The air, the space, the physicality of us has radically changed and new energy, pure creation, and living consciousness is now present and available to us everywhere. In this new sourceness, we discover ultra-connectivity to everything and Life literally comes alive in everything, ourselves included. This is our conscious evolution.

· **Coaching awareness of Living Source Soul** — As Living Source Soul, you're singing the song of Life. It's alchemical. It's in the very fabric of your and our evolving innate beingness. We become it and then automatically alchemically vibrate or sing the song that awakens it in others. It's not making the move for them. Only they can do that. It's alchemically calling it into being. Do they need to know it's happening? Not necessarily, but on some level they do or it wouldn't happen. They have to agree to it on some level of themselves and perhaps we have all already agreed to it simply by being here right now. Maybe that's why we came. It's beyond what wants to happen into the arena of what yearns to happen in us all.

Once this shift has happened for someone you're working with, make them consciously aware of the choice they've just made, what it's all about and how they can live in and as it. In other words, offer them a sustainable interpretation for living in vibrant reality. There are many people who are already there, but they just don't understand what's happened or how they got there. If it feels right, use this framework to help them understand so that they can access their vibrant power with. Otherwise they might still think they're in the old reality and feel stuck in old thought traps. The way to talk about it with another is through the exploration of the feelings of it, rather than an intellectual explanation of it, although both may be required.

EXPERIENTIAL PRACTICE: GETTING IT OUT THERE

· Expand into the living mind and become the Living Soul. Step into it if you don't feel you can become it yet. From here, visualise that you're standing at the doorway to your eternal internal self and hear the Living Source Soul song being sung. Feel it. Don't try to hear with your ears or mind. Now allow the breakthrough to happen and become the living source soul. How does that feel?

· Work with someone you know, a client, a buddy in this course, a friend or family member who's willing to play in this arena now. Move them from Soul to Living Soul and from essence to essentiALLity and discover your own unique ways of making this happen. Each and every one of us will have amazing ways of getting this to breakthrough.

· Once you have the sense of being this Living Source Soul, try vibrating this into being for someone else. Actually, it may already be done for everyone, as we all did that in the breakthrough section. So play with this and see where it wants to take you and us next. We're inviting you to step into the evolution of this, not just to practice it.

BREAKTHROUGH

The enormous breakthrough of this chapter is the discovery of our link to a whole new source energy that is sourcing our brand new, emerging world. The breakthrough is that the whole of humanity can break through to this new sourceness as a living reality. In the moment of this writing, we are connecting with each and every one of you reading this and dancing in this evolutionary dance to sing the source song into vibrant living reality for us all.

CHAPTER FOUR
BEYOND BREAKTHROUGH...
REALITY CREATION EXTRAORDINAIRE

Intention Of This Chapter
- To really get how we create our reality.
- To coach others in reality creation

Profound Potential
- To discover the magical, synergistic, abundant, connective dance of sourcing reality creation.

Key Elements

1 — What is the difference between manifestation and reality creation?
The movement from "I" through "we" to being uniquely "All"

2 — What happens with your energy when you reality-create
Stepping beyond thoughts and intentions into sourcing reality

3 — Seeing big
Making supra-creation a living reality

Exploratory Discussion
1. How do you currently manifest or reality create?
2. Have you had the experience of moving from individual to collective reality creation? If so, what has been the impact?
3. Have you observed that whatever you believe, as the coach, can colour or create your clients' experience?
4. Are you a conscious creator of world reality? If yes, how are you doing that?

ESSENTIAL CONTENT

In the last chapter, we talked about the move from soul to Living Source Soul and from essence to essentiALLity. In this chapter, we're going to take this movement into the levels of reality creation—from the old techniques of manifestation to newly evolving reAllity creation. It's about applying the power of Living Source Soul into the reality of living and evolving Life.

1 — What is the difference between manifestation and reality creation?

Manifestation tends to be about what "I" want. It's about desire. Manifestation feels like engaging personal energy, personal power, and personal will to make something happen that doesn't seem to be happening on its own. At its foundation is "what isn't." Affirmations, positive thinking, and visualisations are some of the techniques that are used in manifestation, but you can see that these are all done from the foundation of what isn't working now and what you want instead.

Reality creation is about what wants to happen on a bigger and greater scale. Traditional reality creation has been about becoming responsible for being a creator: I am a creator of my own and our reality. The foundation lies in being more responsible for what you're thinking and believing and what you put out in your energy creations, consciously and unconsciously. With reality creation you are working more graciously and energetically, in flow. You are beginning to move beyond what the "I" wants and towards what the collective "we" wants. You're serving a greater purpose and taking more conscious responsibility.

Sourcing reality creation orients from a completely new place. It's about living as source sourcing sourceness, creating creation, evolving evolution. You do it from and for All and with and for Life. Its foundational essence is Life and in sourcing creation, you become Life living itself. The orientation here is completely different. It's not even just about the world; it's beyond that. It's about All-ness and beyond. But it's not overwhelming in its size and energy. It actually feels very natural and easy to reAllity create, because in essence that's what you're doing: you're creating reAllity as and for ALL. It's supra-creation!

You can see that these three levels are linked to the levels of self, greater self, and evolutionary self as well as potential, greater potential and evolutionary potential. You are moving from "I" through "we" to being uniquely "All."

2 — What happens with your energy when you reality-create?

When you work with manifestation, your energy is anchored in what you don't want while striving for what you do want. Although you try to keep the focus on what you do want, you are often pulled back into thinking about what you don't want. Given that your underlying thoughts and beliefs are what shape your reality outcome, then manifestation energy can actually create the opposite of what you think you want.

As you make the move to conscious reality creation, you begin to explore those underlying thoughts and beliefs to alter and transform them in a way that will create a more powerful reality outcome for what wants to happen. This creates an opening for easily setting aside what you want and moving into a full and powerful relationship with what wants to happen through you now. Here you surrender your beliefs and desires to steward the powerful energy of creation and potential through, allowing the reality creation to occur with much more ease and grace.

Intention creates the space for the energy of potential to be brought into play. It opens up the possibilities and calls the game into play. But is intention alone sufficient to initiate reality creation? Some people would say yes, but we're not certain that's true in every case. If, as you set your intention, you fully and completely believe that what you are intending IS an absolute reality for you now, then it will be so. It will come into your reality. But that's not just because you set an intention for it, it's because you know that it is already a fully realised reality. If you're setting an intention on top of wanting it to be some other way than it is, the reality that creates will be what you really believe it is.

We're talking about moving beyond static thoughts and beliefs and beyond intention setting built on a reality of how you know it is and what you'd like it to be. We are talking about moving to a place where all the energy for potential that you create is already a living reality for you and us now. It's almost like you have to be willing to be the alchemical eyes of reality and as you see it, so it is. It's a fluid, dynamic, alchemical dance that lightly creates a brand new reality. We're inviting you to understand that "as you see it, so it is." The observer is the creator and it is time we took responsibility for that. But even more than that, it's time we evolve that power to the next levels of reality creation.

The evolution of reality creation occurs when you move from personal reality creation to sourcing reality creation. Personal reality creation is you saying what you want to happen, using your own energy to make that so, and intending it just for you and the reality around you. Personal reality creation is wonderful and fulfilling, but it doesn't necessarily evolve Life and All as it occurs.

In sourcing reality creation, you reality-create inside the energy of All. More than just an observer/ creator, you become source sourcing sourceness. The energetic focus is All and what wants to be now, as opposed to your own energy fields and what you want now in reality creation.

When you move to the unique experience of being All, you move beyond thoughts, beliefs, and intentions. It's like they don't exist anymore. From this vantage point, you see that you can believe anything you want at any time, and that thoughts, beliefs, and intentions are actually irrelevant to the movement. In fact, thoughts, beliefs, and intentions can actually slow up or curtail the movement.

When you are working purely with the energy in a clear, alchemical state, you are free flowing in the dance of creation. You surrender to the dance and there is no difference between you and it. The energy is sourcing the movement of the potential into reality through your experience and expression of Life. You become all of it and you source the movement, the dance, and the potential moving into being.

The analogy here is like Neo in The Matrix. Once you realise that reality is only a construct of thoughts, beliefs, and intentions that people think is real, then the freedom to invent and evolve reality in every moment is available to you. It's beyond just being responsible for your thoughts, beliefs, and intentions. It's as if there are no thoughts, beliefs, constructs, or frameworks in this space. It's as if you are a master programmer alchemically co-creating the dance of creation with other master programmers who are already in the dance with you. You may not know, as you're in the throes of creating, the reality that you're sourcing and creating. On some level of yourself you do know, but on another level you're simply in the alchemical dance, discovering its amazing unfoldment as you flow. At the same time, you are the alchemical ingredient that makes it all come real. Without you, it wouldn't be so.

If you're in your mind, thinking, believing or intending, then you are reality creating, but not in an alchemical way. What you think, believe, and intend moves the energy into that perspective of reality... and so it is. When you are sourcing reality creation you are moving into the alchemical dance where you're working beyond thoughts, beliefs and intentions. Your mind is not engaged. So what is engaged then? The Living Mind and Living Soul in partnership with you, consciousness, creation, and more, all married together into one dynamic process. You make the shift from you as a personal energy with thoughts, beliefs and intentions trying to responsibly and consciously create reality to you as a being operating as the energy of All and knowingly sourcing the reality dance.

As one being working as All and working with what Life and All wants, you have the possibility of re-creating the whole of reality in an instant. This might raise tons of questions from the "I" perspective, but not necessarily from the All perspective. Why is that? Because you're working as source sourcing sourceness and so you sense, feel, and know that you're working with what Life wants. If you tried to do anything that was contrary to Life and All, it wouldn't work. In this space, you actually find that you don't want to do anything other than what Life and All wants because you and the movement are so in synch with the evolving cosmos. And even if you tried to make something happen, but isn't what Life and ALL wants, it likely wouldn't occur.

You experience and become brilliant, creative flow.

What happens with personal desire in this place? It gets supplanted by a passionate desire for Life because that's what brings everything alive. From here, you can get more than you can personally desire on the level of self. Life for you, others and the world becomes a lot better than you can even imagine. In the end, you actually do end up getting what you want, albeit in more expanded and creative ways than you could have imagined.

Sourcing reality creation used to be done (and still can be if you choose this) from expanded All consciousness. You go out to the pure place of consciousness and seed potential/creation into play and then intend it into living reality. However, in recent months, a new option or movement has been brought into play. Since the marriage of Living Mind and Living Soul and the marriage of consciousness and creation, the movement now occurs right in the spaces in front of you and inside of you. It is more present. It occurs with a simple breath. In fact, it is often now instantaneous.

Sourcing reality creation used to be experienced as pulling potential out of the warehouse of creation and seeding it into consciousness and then drawing it into living reality. But now, with our present relationship with new sourceness in the air around us and as us, we simply feel the rightness of what wants to be created now and super-charge the air around us, knowing that it is done and it is already so. It is as if the reality that was before that moment no longer exists. It disappears from your energy fields, from your mind, from your beliefs and from your reality. It is instantly what is so because you are fully experiencing it as your true reality. And more than that, you have super-charged the whole of reality with it so people are feeding back to you this shift without them knowing quite how that happened. You didn't do it to them. You simply were the initiator, the evocateur for the potential of what wanted to alchemically become real.

When sourcing reality, it's an all-permeating, all pervading holistic experience of Life living itself to the fullest. When you do it, it's done for everything, everywhere. Built into what you create is its own evolution. This is because the potential you're alchemising has its own source consciousness built into it. The potential is as much alive and conscious as you are. This isn't your personal creation. It's a source creation. You do own the responsibility of sourcing the movement, but you don't own the actual creation. It has a life of its own and is already fully alive as you super-charge it into being. You're more than a catalyst because you are sourcing it. You're more than just a person who picked it up and charged it into being. Without you, it may never have come to be. You bring your essentiALL uniqueness to the game and make it like no one else could.

Once you've sourced something into being, you don't necessarily need to steward it or be responsible for it over time. And you can't hold on to it because that can limit its dance. When sourcing reality creation, it comes alive and has a built-in consciousness of its own, which then enters into a dance with all other conscious creators to continually source its evolution from their essentiALL uniqueness. You will sense, feel, and know when to let go and allow others to do their part and you'll know when to continue to source its movement. It will feel really right for you to do. It's like an evolving dance of creation—you dance and move on, dance and move on, dance and move on.

3 — Seeing big

When you're in Living Soul, integrated with Living Mind, and connected to limitless possibilities that source from every point around you and within you, you see from a different place. You see BIG and are able to source reality creation beyond anything that your own eyes could see or your own mind could imagine.

What if you expanded your conscious awareness to be as big as all the cosmoses and took a look at the movement of all consciousness through all the levels everywhere? What do you see? How big are you seeing from?

There's something about this exercise that puts you in touch with the bigger game. It's supra-consciousness supra-creating. We can walk around with our eyes wide open and be connected with the biggest, vastest, deepest view of everything that we choose to see.

Why stop with just a personal or an Earth view? Why not look bigger to see how it all fits together into a grand, amazing, evolutionary board game with omni-dimensional levels? When you look from this vantage point, you move into an alchemical state where your eyes, your breath, and your energy are all source initiators for reality to burst into being.

If you're the eyes of everything and All seeing massively big—bigger than the Earth and bigger than this thriving cosmos— and if you know that as you see it so it is, how would you dance with your alchemicALL eyes? As you see, so you reality-create.

Maybe reality creation isn't such a cumbersome process anymore. Maybe it's simple and delightful because the power is in your seeing. It's not just about perception. It's about altering what is into what can be as you observe it and catalyse it. You're its initiator and evocateur. You make it real by being willing to see it so. It all happens from a very light place.

There is a relationship, or perhaps better said, a partnership with the rightness of what wants to be reality-created right here right now. Whatever comes through you to be created will automatically be for you as well as for All. It's because of your passion, your personal desire, and your essentiALL uniqueness that draws this potential to you to be done for All. And so, you become the one to reality create that for yourself, others and ALL.

Try it out. Allow what wants to be reality created to pop up as a feeling of rightness. If you have to think about it, reconsider. Instead, expand, allow yourself to connect with new Life source within and around you, and then simply allow the rightness of the reality to be created, to be super-charged into being. Then simply make it so. This is supra creation. It's like waving a magic wand.

Once this new reAllity you've created is really present and available, it automatically flows into the connected consciousness of us all. For example, suppose someone moved from a belief that there were no great guys out there to be in relationship with to a true and powerful knowing and seeing of mega men available everywhere. Does this then affect everyone? Well, yes it does, but it depends on how far and wide that person believes it to be so. If they believe that's the true nature of men and relationships now, then that's what shows up everywhere around them as well as what begins to appear in the conscious living of others throughout the world. For those that are already living in vibrant reality, they will instantly feel the shift and accept this as their new reality as well because they're in touch with and living what Life wants as well. When we reality create on this level, it's actually happening in the new collective consciousness, so it is automatically available to All. If someone is closed and perhaps in old or middle paradigm reality with a set of beliefs that preclude this from being so, it's possible that they can separate themselves from this shift and not experience it as so, even though it is. But even though they're experiencing this from a place of closedness, there will be influencing energetics in the air surrounding them, calling them into this newest new. An alchemical process may be beginning for them and, to use our example, suddenly great guys begin to show up. That's because there's more space given for them to show up as "great" and they're called into becoming, into evolving their potential. Then, the reality becomes its own proof.

How is this beyond breakthrough as the title of this chapter implies? In breakthrough, there is an edgy, sharp, laser-like movement from one stuck place to a newly emerging place. But what we're talking about here has no stuck place to move from. You're alchemising into being what already is right there waiting and wanting to be. Breakthrough takes more energy, albeit vibrant and amazing energy, whereas supra-reality creating is a simple alchemical ping and then it is so. It is an ecstatic movement of being and becoming. You experience this reality as already so, like a vibrant, alchemical bliss state or a harmonic code that's very light and right, and that zings it into true and powerful being.

Once you've become source sourcing sourceness, it is a living reality. You begin to see it and discover it everywhere. You also discover that there are no old or negative thoughts left associated with what was before. There's only the new as the reality continually evolves. Built into supra reality creation is its own evolution.

Exercise

· **Coaching another to supra reality create** –

1. Have them breathe, relax and expand their energy.
2. Ask them to move their focus of attention from the mind to the Living Mind and from the soul to the Living Soul. There's a real sense of moving from sensing things inside themselves to being super-connected to everything around then. If this language doent work for the client, you can suggest that they expand into the bigger, deeper levels of themselves that they do know exist somewhere in their conscious awareness. They may not be always living on these levels, but almost everyone is in touch at some point with these levels of themselves. You can also use some of the exercises in previous chapters for this step.
3. Ask them to feel their connection to new Life Source energy. Another way to say this is to connect with Life with a capital L. Have them allow this energy to flow through them from their own source connection. And then, ask them to connect their source flow into the greater source flow that exists all around us.
4. Next, have them feel the rightness of what wants to pop up for them to reality create right now. Invite them to have no thoughts about what that might be, but to simply be in touch with the alchemical dance of new creation and move into its song and motion.
5. Whatever comes up as potential, have them reach the energy of it out through them to super charge the air with it. It's an activation, a breath of creation. It has its own motivation and momentum and they get to be its supra creator.
6. Have them experience the full feeling of being a supra-creator. This is really important. It's almost like the alchemical experience of it solidifies it in the reality. So have them feel it and infuse it in every cell and in everything around them. Affirm its being. Welcome it into living reality.
7. Finally, have them look to see if they have any old or negative thoughts left around. They shouldn't dig deep for them or try to recreate the old. Instead, just do a quick check of how they're feeling and thinking now. They should discover that the old thoughts and beliefs are gone, like magic, and only the new exists in that moment.

· **Coaching through remaining old thoughts and beliefs** – What if after the exercise above the client still has lingering old thoughts and beliefs? Perhaps they chose the thing to reality create and what they chose didn't come from that rightness of timing or lightness of being. If that's the case, simply have them go back and get the right thing for them for this moment. You can also check to see if they're acting from a really connected place and if not, recheck the connections and find where it needs to move to be fully alchemically available for them. Ask them to retry the exercise in their own natural way to do it. Perhaps there's something different for them, that makes it more instinctively happen with them in a unique way.

There could also be a fundamental belief that says either "I can't do this" or "human beings can't do this" or that asks, "is it right for us to do?" Sourcing reality creation is a fairly major shift for humanity. Before we were creating, but we were mostly doing it negatively and unconsciously. Now we have the opportunity to supra-create in a fully conscious, connected, whole, and expanded state. Play with them around their belief system and what they choose to believe right now. It's not about getting them to believe something. It's more about simply questioning and shedding light on what they believe to see if it empowers and supports them. Be light about it and loosen up the beliefs for them to grow into where they need to be in the moment.

If there is a fundamental existing belief that won't shift and that is in the way of what really wants to happen, then they're very likely back in their mind and thinking. When you're fully connected to the Living Mind and Living Soul, there's an integral connection to Life and the experience seems to happen more naturally. Beliefs don't tend to come up at all. The energy of the reality that you want to supra-create simply won't happen from a disconnected space. So again make sure that they're ultra-connected.

EXPERIENTIAL PRACTICE: GETTING IT OUT THERE

· Go play. Be light about it. Have fun knowing that you are the supra reality creator sourcing our newest new reality into being. Try it on everything: abundance, healthy living, relationships, new work, and so on. Etc. From this new place, everything is possible and Life is a delightful, ongoing mega-creation. Discover this power in yourself and in all those you coach and touch as you dance through Life.

· Try it for yourself several times before you coach it in another. Make sure you have a real experience of it before trying it with someone else. If you're uncertain, it won't work for them. Why? Because you're such a powerful reality creator. Once you're comfortable with it and have it in your experience, then, take someone you're coaching and have them try the different levels of reality creation (manifestation, reality creation and sourcing reality creation) and dance in the process together and see what you and they discover.

· If you're working on something that's really, really big and it feels bigger than even you as All can do, then call on the collective to do it with you. By collective, we don't mean call on everyone in the world necessarily. It's more about calling those resonant others who are ready to share in this particular creation at this moment. You can call on the whole of humanity if that feels right to do, but make sure that you're calling on the mega / source level of them, not the physical, day-to-day level that actually might disorient the energetics of what you're about to bring through. When you collectively create the same reality, it makes it more powerful and lighter. It has more charge to it and more delivery associated with it. This will be one of the focuses of our third course: AlchemicAll Power.

BREAKTHROUGH

The breakthrough for this chapter is for supra-reality creation to become a natural state of being for all. As we tuned in to this reality, we connected with all of you and sourced it into being.

CHAPTER V
SOURCING AND COACHING VIBRANT, CREATIVE GENIUS

Intention Of This Chapter
- To be able to coach and source genius in yourself and in others on unprecedented levels.
- To be able to coach and source super-creativity, original thinking, and visionary living in yourself and others.

Profound Potential
- To discover the powerful potential of Living Mind married with Living Soul.
- To think, act, and create like never before and in the act of doing so, to evolve creative genius.

Key Elements
1 — New creative genius
How is it evolving and where is it evolving to?
2 — Sourcing the evolution of vibrant, creative genius
Your role in our collective evolution

Exploratory Discussion
1. Have you ever accessed human genius for yourself?
If yes, how did you do that and how did it feel? Are you able to recreate that experience?
2. How do you access creativity and what do you think is its relationship to genius?
3. What do you currently believe about the state of human genius and the possibilities around our evolution?

ESSENTIAL CONTENT

1 — New creative genius

Is human genius a fluke of genes for the predestined few or is it something that every single person has access to in varying, unique ways?

In the past human genius was considered a privilege of the small minority who were born with exceptional abilities. These geniuses appeared to operate in some way that was different to normal human ability. The general consensus has been that the average person doesn't have access to genius, to being a great thinker, to unprecedented inventions, to seeing beyond what is to something greater and more powerful.

We've tried to measure genius in people through IQ tests but the true source of genius doesn't necessarily come from mind. In fact, the original meaning of genius did make the connection to a greater source of information: the Living Mind. Perhaps our culture's interpretation of genius has been limited and we've not sought, encouraged and empowered that inherent genius innate within everyone.

We believe any one in any moment can access original thinking, evolutionary inventiveness, and super-creativity. Everyone has something magnificently special that is their own unique genius inside of them. This genius as a way of being is available to all of us now even though we may apply our genius in different ways (e.g. carpentry, gardening, cooking, philosophy, consciousness work, and so on).

Human genius is evolving. There is an emerging, creative evolution of human intelligence and ability that allows us to more easily access and celebrate genius in every one. As we marry Living Mind with Living Soul—or knowing and wisdom with super-creation—what we get is this new, vibrant, creative genius.

In The Living Mind course, we moved from the mind into the Living Mind. We took a step from inside ourselves to outside ourselves to connect with living intelligence. Vibrant, creative genius is about evolving that step, about bringing the Living Mind into yourself, into every cell. What if every cell in your body and in the air all around us is full and rich with this vibrant, creative genius? If that's so, then all we have to do is to embrace it in its fullest.

The Living Mind, through its marriage to Living Soul, naturally evolves into living, vibrant, creative genius. In the past, wisdom was like a library; a static storage place where you went to access the information. In the Living Mind, the information is more active and participative with us, giving us access to new intelligence and new ways to be. In living genius, it seems that living intelligence has taken on a sentient, alchemical partnership with us, which gifts us vibrant, creative, inventive genius beyond anything we've experienced before. We're now in full relationship with Life and All and with the full genius of all potential and possibility realising itself.

This is about an evolution of the Living Mind into an alchemical, thriving, pulsing, inventive and creative genius. What if from this point forward, every single being actually lives within, and as, the ocean of alchemical genius? How is Life different from here?

We live inside evolving belief.
We source creation in any moment.
We think super-originally, evolving thinking beyond what is, and has been, to unprecedented new ways.
We're inventive, coming up with new solutions that have never been considered before.
We live in alchemical knowing with vibrancy, dynamism, clarity and confidence.
We are more leaderful and have no fixed agenda for how anything has to go. We see potential in every moment and empower inventive, creative genius in every person we touch.

In the future, collaborative genius ("geniUS") will also become available to us. In other words, whatever is available to one will be available to all. It's possible we may all be working as one magnificent super-brain, sharing genius capacity and potential. We will be further exploring collective geniUs in course three of Advanced Coach Training.

If anyone can access all wisdom, knowledge, learning and creativity, then our relationship to education and learning completely alters. No longer needing to stuff facts into our brains to store for future memory, we can live free and ultra-connected in the moment to access anything we want to know from any time, place, or consciousness. And more than that, there's a fluid, alchemical support system available through the inter-connectivity of self, mind, and being with living genius. This revolutionises the human learning experience. It allows us to evolve the concept of learning from static information and learning from mistakes to living alchemical information and gracious learning as an output of evolution. Learning becomes a journey of experiential discovery and a gracious unfoldment of what Life wants next. It's ever evolving. You alchemise what Life wants and learning wondrously occurs as an output of the evolutionary movement.

Vibrant, creative genius is fully integrated with the Living Mind and profoundly lives in and as the Living Soul. It is the marriage of living consciousness and Life's creational, generational ability to thrive and pulse into new realms and ways of being. It lives in the moment inside every cell of every being and every thing. It is the essential source quality of Life sourcing Life.

Vibrant, creative genius is the ability to think originally and inventively, to live fully present, to create creation, and to alter Life with every thought and breath. It is related to the vibrancy of and connectivity with Life. It is a state of being, a way of living in a super-charged state. You can choose to move into a state of genius at any moment.

Vibrant, creative genius is exhilarating. It goes beyond thinking or an isolated experience of the mind trying to understand things. With this new genius, there isn't the same need to understand how and why, but more a sense of knowing a thing or a concept from its inventive, creative source and then seeing where and how that can be enhanced, enlivened and evolved. It's a pulsing, thriving genius that's very active and alchemical. It marries the wisdom of the ages with the generative wisdom of the moment to produce a new experience and expression of genius. This allows us to invent Life anew and to access new possibilities for our evolution.

Vibrant, creative genius sources inventiveness. It's about being able to see and think way beyond what is to create and evolve from new abundant possibilities that sparkle in the air around us and in the cells within us. When you consciously become this vibrant, new, creative genius, your outlook on Life really changes. You become oriented to Life and your perception of things alters completely. You no longer see from the small human eyes, but instead become the alchemicALL eyes that see and inspire creative movement everywhere with great ease and grace.

We have already co-created this new level of enhanced intelligence and now we're learning to live as it. There's a whole shift from individual intelligence and genius in the mind to a holistic field of inventive and creative possibility that you, and we, are constantly re-sourcing.

Exercises

· **Coaching vibrant, creative genius in others** –

1. Ask your clients if that's what they want: to be vibrant, creative geniuses. Not everyone is going to want to do this immediately, so tune in and be sure the timing is right for them to take this step. But also remember that each of us is capable of genius and the more you see this as true and live it yourself, the more others will willingly step into it too.
2. Be sure to check how open they are and whether they're in wholeness and / or beyond, or not. Especially make sure the high heart is open before you do all this work. You can check out their energetic state by (1) asking them how they're experiencing it, (2) pretending to be them to see how their energy feels and flows and (3) tuning in to your knowing about it to see where they're open and where they're not (e.g. head, heart, high heart, spirit, soul/whole). If they're not open, ask them to think about something they're passionate about; that should open them to wholeness. If this doesn't work, then go through the exercises in the roadmap to wholeness in chapter one of this course. Your goal is to get them to move through open and whole into the readiness to integrate Living Soul / Living Mind. This can be done in no time at all if you don't make a big deal of it or think that's it's more complex than it is. It can be done in seconds or minutes but sometimes can take a bit longer. Just make sure that you as a coach are not in the way of the process by what you believe. If you will them to be there graciously and easily, so it will be. This step into wholeness, and then beyond it, is an ongoing movement of energetic becoming that will continue beyond your coaching session with this person. Remember that what you're coaching here is the energetic movement and integration, which can supported by conversation around their intentions and what they believe, but is actually more about stepping into a brand new way to be as a human being. And that's a willingness to co-create our human evolution.
3. The next step is to reframe for them how human genius occurs, so that they can see that something new is available to them now. If they hold genius as we've held it in the past, they'll likely think it's impossible for them. As a way of playing with it, have them imagine themselves as an evolving kind of genius. Let it take imaginary shape for them in their energetic experience. Play with it lightly. Don't make this serious and significant. Have them step beyond themselves to imagine that they could operate in

a new genius and then act as if that was so. Make sure they're in an expanded energy experience as they do this. As they free flow and play with it, this new genius will become more of their living experience.

4. Ask them to feel their energetic connection to creation, or ask them to experience themselves as creation. n whatever way that feels right for them now, have them bring creation more present and fully connect with creational potential in every cell. At one point in time, creation seemed to be a distinct place where potential and possibilities were stored waiting for birth. But today, creation seems to abound all around us and is interwoven with consciousness and Life. Creation now permeates everything and can occur as a living experience exploding and imploding into everything everywhere. This is actually the integration of Living Mind and Living Soul. But you don't have to do this as the distinct steps of moving into Living Mind and intending Living Soul. It can be much more fluid than that. As you're going through this process of bringing creation present, integration naturally occurs. The infusion of new creational possibility with the cellular structure of the body and the dynamic evolution of the brain into a more open, fluid, creational, alchemical state gives you the marriage of living mind and living soul. So what we're really saying is simple: Have them become new creation walking.

5. So far in this process, they've said yes they want it, they're open to the motion of becoming as part of our human evolution, they're open to the concept of new creative genius, and they've brought creation present in their cells and minds. Next, ask them to become new, vibrant, creative genius walking. Free up the thoughts and beliefs that might be blocking them from doing so. Keep in mind that it also might not be the right timing for them, so allow for that as well. This person has to be willing to move into this becoming by their own conscious choosing. As an evolutionary coach, the more you step into this becoming yourself, the easier it will be for your clients to make the move. It becomes natural, even though initially it might seem like the most outrageous and unprecedented step for people to take.

6. Once they've accepted and become the energy of new, vibrant, creative genius, the next step is to get them in touch with and aligned to the vibrant power of this creative genius. Once they can say to themselves, "I am new, vibrant, creative genius" something alchemical automatically happens. Movement begins immediately. Every cell fills with a super-charging energy and you become a vast, interconnected, inspirational movement that is Living Soul / Living Mind dancing in the moment. You discover here an enhanced capacity for creational alchemy. Encourage them to play here, to revel in it and to be light about it. This isn't something they need to learn how to do. It's naturally available to them from this becoming. It's really more about enjoying the exploration of living it than it is trying to reorient to doing something new.

7. Support them in understanding how Life changes from this point on. For example, their relationship to learning and working with emotions may change and they will find themselves able to invent new ideas with greater ease, which will mean more fluidity in the movement of their work. Give them a basis for being able to integrate this

genius into daily activities by applying it to the projects they're at work on. Show them how to bring super-creativity into their everyday lives and all that they do.

a. Have them take a few minutes each day to tune in to creation and see what wants to happen through them.

b. Ask them to stop when they're uncertain about things and use those moments to gain super-creative clarity for how to go forward.

c. If they're seeking creativity for a particular purpose, show them how to move from their minds to Living Mind to open to all manner of new ideas and concepts and to let the energy flow. Work with them to think inventively and originally. This might take a little bit of practice as we re-orient ourselves from static thinking to vibrant, creative thinking beyond what is known. In vibrant creativity you are focusing on the new and this is where huge leaps in thinking can occur.

d. Guide them to really focus on freshness and newness and to observe when thinking is occurring statically. Have them catch themselves every time they think or say 'this is the way things are.' That's a static thought, not an evolving, creational, alchemical possibility. This will guide them to live more continuously in the ultra-creative moment. Here, they're more aligned with evolutionary potential and this potential becomes the evocation that inspires creative action. You begin to work for evolution as an alchemical, creational motion and therefore the impact on the world and others occurs very naturally and graciously, and is beyond any expectations that we could normally imagine.

2 — Sourcing the evolution of vibrant, creative genius

Once you become vibrant, creative genius, you'll discover that you begin to work in new and alchemical ways that may occur to you in every moment. You don't ever get stuck in "this is the way it is." You're forever inventing the new.

But beyond that even, there is a point at which you accept yourself as an evolver of creative genius. This is where the evolution of humanity really comes into play.

Are you willing to be an evolver of human genius? Can you see this is a different question than becoming or living as new, creative genius?'

Take it on to see how it feels. Try owning that you are THE evolver of human genius, along with all the others around the world and beyond who are co- generating this evolution, and see what happens from this place of ultimate responsibility of us turning out brilliantly brand new. What do you discover when you become the source of genius? It lends a whole new flavour and levels of possibility to the evolutionary dance.

Exercise

· **Becoming creative genius** – To become vibrant, creative genius in your everyday life, you must operate as All re-inventing itself and Life sourcing itself anew in every moment. Orient your mental, emotional, and energetic processes to reinvention and evolution. Re-orient yourself to believing and knowing that you can access the genius of All. Allow yourself to believe that it is there for us all. You don't have to go anywhere to get it; it is already with us now. If you're at all uncertain about that, then expand into the Living Mind, connect yourself with Life, and intend to experience living, vibrant, creative genius for a minute. See how it feels. Play with it, dance in it, try it out in a variety of different ways that suit you.

EXPERIENTIAL PRACTICE: GETTING IT OUT THERE

· Move yourself into a fully open and vibrant state and intend to access the new, vibrant, creative genius. How does it feel? What do you discover as you do this?

· Apply this new genius to a project, like discovering a new name for something or coming with a new idea on something you're passionate about. Bring any problems or challenges you're experiencing into the creative genius dance and see how problem solving is altered.

· Ask yourself if you are willing to live as 'a' or 'the' evolver of human genius and see what comes up around that. If being an evolver of human genius isn't your specialty, then pick the speciality that is yours. What are you ultimately responsible for in regards to our collective evolution? This is a profound discovery process through which you'll really get to see who you are willing to be for the world and beyond. Don't get caught up in the burden of taking on big things. Remember that in the new, you can do your work in no time at all and with a lot of grace and ease.

· Choose one friend or client that you can take through this process of becoming new, vibrant, creative genius and try it out on them. Or choose a buddy in the course and work on it to take each other through into vibrant, creative genius.

· Discover living as this new creative genius and play with working in collective consciousness with your course group or with others around the world who share this vision. Discover the brand new, ever-evolving, collaborative, alchemical geniUS.

BREAKTHROUGH

The breakthrough of this chapter is to move beyond being and coaching creative genius into evolving creative genius, consciousness, and more. It's about you stepping into the full, creative, alchemical power of sourcing Life. Imagine if we can all do this, what the implications are for our world!

CHAPTER VI
THE POWER OF LIVING SOUL

Intention Of This Chapter
- To fully step into and become the power of Living Soul.
- To live vibrantly and creatively as the power of Living Soul.
- To co-create new levels of power.
- To coach, evoke, and empower new levels of power for those we work with.

Profound Potential
- To take coaching beyond coaching and into powerful alchemical evocation.

Key Elements

1 — The Power of Living Soul
The journey to date

2 — Accessing levels of leadership and power
Moving and coaching through to alchemical power

Exploratory Discussion

1. How do you access and define your power?
2. How do you experience your power in Living Soul? Is your experience changing?
3. Have you experienced an increase in your access to power since you started this programme?
4. How do you see your power and the power of Living Soul evolving?

ESSENTIAL CONTENT

1 — The Power of Living Soul

We began this course with a look at the roadmap to wholeness through the integration of head, heart, spirit, and soul. Next, we made the shift from soul to Living Soul. As Living Soul, we moved from essence to essentiALLity—from being to brilliant, unique, innate being and from soul to Living Source Soul.

In other words, we have been experiencing the evolution of humanity. Advanced Coach Training is about the evolution of human consciousness, taking what it is to be human to entirely new levels.

We then alchemised new levels of reality creation and discovered how we can graciously and alchemically move the evolving new into living reality. We discovered sourcing sourceness, creating creation, and evolving evolution as a way of living Life. From here, we opened up the access to evolving intelligence (the marriage of Living Mind and Living Soul) into a vibrant, creative, new genius.

The next step is weaving this all together and putting it into play, into the power of Living Soul. To arrive at the real power of Living Soul, let's look at the various levels of power to see how they are evolving.

Power over – Power has traditionally been defined as "power over another." It has been about controlling and dominating, where one person or group gets another or others to do what they want them to. It's hierarchical and doesn't recognise the beauty of the whole. It's power *over* as opposed to *inclusive, co-creative* power.

No power – Way back when (we're talking millennia ago) as we moved into the closed energy state, people lost their ability to access their own inner and external knowing and guidance. We looked to others to give us that guidance, and often whoever might had the loudest, clearest voice were those practicing "power over." We were exploring power in its extremes, like a pendulum swing. We had to delve into the full depths of "no power" in order to make our way to the evolution of power for all.

Not playing in the game – Recently, a new kind of power has emerged where we remove ourselves from the game. We say no to the systems approach to power and move away from traditional jobs and professions to create new ways to play. This is in itself a form of power. In fact, all of us who've stopped playing in the game of traditional power, have given ourselves the opportunity to invent ways of accessing and living a new kind of power.

Soft power – As we began to invent new kinds of power, we co-created an evolution of power. We discovered new ways to dance powerfully. One of these new kinds of power is soft power. It works gently to hold space, heal, bring through the light, and love things into being. If you are working in this way, you can play in the background without the need to be seen and known as the one doing it. You do it gently and graciously for all.

Empowerment – Next came empowerment of self and others. With the evolution of power, we began to recognise the equality of each other's power, to empower all types of power. It is the recognition of power in others that brings it into being. Traditional leadership has been about control, but new leadership is about being leaderful. You have leaderful people who empower collaborative co-creation from a place of unique offerings and a recognition of each person's contribution to the whole. As you become empowered yourself, you begin to naturally empower others.

Creational power – Also known as vibrant power, this is where power comes alive. It sparks through in and out of everything you do. It's not about deciding to be in your power one moment and not the next. It's about living wholly and creationally. It's about working with the levels of potential to take us beyond where we are, beyond what is, to the levels of what can be. It's alchemical in nature and orients us to a bigger "we" and to a vibrant connection with Life. The sense of power comes from that vibrant connection with the newly evolving Life source energy. It pours out of you. You become a fountain, or a wellspring, for vibrant Life source and for super-creativity.

Alchemical power – Beyond creational power, this is where you take the step into uniquely becoming the Living Source Soul. More than becoming one with All and then doing whatever All wants, it is about super-connecting with the richly evolving fabric of All-ness and bringing your unique essentiALLity (evolving purpose and reason for being) to the dance of evolutionary co-creation. The full expression of power here is in the connectivity to All-ness, to your essentiAL uniqueness and to all others who are in the dance of evolutionary co-creation.

Through the energetic shift from creational, vibrant power to alchemical power your connections to everything are remade. In vibrant, creational power you are super-connected to Life and All. But in alchemical power, you become All "All-ing" itself to new levels of being. It's exhilarating in that you are uniquely yourself within it, but you're collaborating with ALL to source things into being, to potentialise potential beyond what wants to be and beyond what we have ever thought it could be.

In vibrant, creational power, you feel extraordinarily energetic, you're a sparkling fountain of energy and creation. But it's you, creation, and the energy of potential at play. In alchemical power, you are integrated with the energy of All that wants to be, dancing with others in collective consciousness to bring it into play. There's a lot more energy and a lot more presence in alchemical power. You step beyond your own individual energy to move into the huge energetic movement of, and for, All. There is a freedom of movement here that's extraordinary.

2 — Accessing levels of leadership and power

Soft power — Soft power is about being whole and working energetically but the thing that's missing from it is the connection to creation. In soft power, it's more about giving the energy presence and then allowing it to do its thing. You're really saying 'I'm not the leader", but you're also making a huge contribution by bringing the energy present. You access soft power by making the move to wholeness and from there, you begin to work in partnership with the energy.

Empowerment — Empowerment is where you start to take responsibility for being a leader, evoking leadership and power in others. You discover the first levels of sourcing power. It doesn't yet require a connection to creation, but it is a step beyond wholeness. The step happens when you actually own your own leadership and your part in the movement of what wants to happen. This is the first affirmation and acknowledgement that your power really exists. The interesting thing about the step into empowerment and empowering is that even though you've owned your leadership, your focus is no longer on you. It is on empowering others to be leaders as well or at least to offer their unique contributions. This is different from traditional leadership where it was normally about you making it all happen. This is where collaboration truly begins.

Creational power — In creational power, you make the connection to and/or become creation, you move you into a different relationship with power. Creational powers is dynamic, spontaneous, and interactive. It's all around you; you're in and of it. The high heart has to be open and you're in vibrant reality, in the Living Soul. You're really connected and from here, you initiate the movement of potential into creation graciously and instinctively.

Alchemical power — The move to alchemical power is a step into full source power. You become the Living Source Soul. It's more than being creational and it's more than being willing to own your own leadership and power. Here, with every breath you take, everything you see, every word you speak, and every move you make, Life evolves. Here, we dance in the power of All. You simply become it and alchemy thrives in everything you do. To step into alchemical power, become Living Soul. Allow this to fill every cell.

As you move to alchemical power, the nature and essence of your work evolves along with you. As you become Living Soul, you also become the power of Living Soul. Alchemy becomes the fabric of everything you are and do and movement occurs very naturally all the time. Alchemical power has an assured presence in you and as you. You are it and you have the full power and strength of All, of Life, and of our evolving collective consciousness. Your power energetically moves way beyond your own personal power or even the power of creation to the power of All.

Once you've stepped into alchemical power, it's always with you. It's alive in you. It's not necessarily something that comes and goes or that you move in or out of. You are the power and you are also of it. You let go of everything you've thought of power in the past and of all that you thought your work was to step fully into a brand new evolving you/us. What you discover here is the completion of you as you've always been, and that allows you to take yourself, and the whole of humanity along with you, to whole new levels. If you try to hang on to who you think you are or what you think your work is, you can hinder the integration of the power. Be prepared to let it all go and move fully into the now moment of becoming.

Alchemical power holds within it a presence of knowing, wisdom, alchemy, creation, and capability. Once you choose to step into it, to own it, then all of that is available to you. There's a real lightness to this power. There's no ego attached to it at all. There's no force in the traditional sense of the word. Alchemical power is liberating for everyone that it touches. It does not feelk serious and significant—but you can do really significant, profound work with it in a vibrant, delightful kind of way.

It's alchemical grace. You might not care how things will turn out and yet you're vibrantly committed to the action that you'll take. There's a new kind of power in this paradox. Alchemical power brings everything much more to action. You don't just do something creational or alchemical, stop, and then wait a few days for the next potential to rise. It's as if you're a constant stream of possibilities moving into reality. It is a becoming and it's not just you becoming. Everything is becoming as you dance in and as alchemical power.

Exercises

· **Coaching different levels of power** — Think of the purpose of soft power as "being creative," vibrant power as "being the breath of creation," and alchemical power as "evolving creation into its next levels of itself." Soft power is used to coach others to live better lives, vibrant power for empowering others to step into bigger levels of their own unique leadership, and alchemical power for 'evolving power and leadership. When you're open to the evolution of you, your work and us, then the movement into alchemical power occurs. You then live that context with every breath of you. You become evolution living and evolving itself.

· **Coaching soft power** — First you want to have them be open to increasing their access to their own power. A lot of people have concerns about the very word power, let alone stepping into more. You want to talk about the concept of power and get them comfortable with and ready to open up to something new around it. The move to soft power is a wonderful step on the journey to wholeness. It's very appealing because of its nurturing nature and because it has no focus on the need to be seen or known as the leader. It's also the first step to experiencing and working with energy. Soft power is actually a form of energetic power. It's where the person and the energy move into a partnership dance. To support your clients in accessing soft power:

1. First show them how to open their heart and high heart.
2. Next, see if they are still keeping themselves (their soul) protectively inside and if yes, have them bring the inner out into the light of day and discover its strength.
3. Have them expand their energy and allow the feeling of wholeness and of the flow of their own personal energy to initiate. Holding the soul in restricts the flow of personal and creative energy through the physical.

4. Now, ask them to experience their own energy. They may feel more tingling in their hands, through their heart area, and even throughout the whole body. They may just feel infinitely more alive.

5. Next, have them experience energy—not just their own but the energetic levels that surround us. This is where an understanding of vibrant energetics is helpful. As they open up, you want to make sure that they move into *vigorous* open as opposed to *vulnerable* open. Vigorous open is where the heart and high heart are open, the soul is flipped out, and they're connected to Life. Vulnerable open is where only the heart is open and they're sitting there wide open to everything that comes along.

6. Now show them how to work energetically. Let's use holding space for someone as an example of wonderful soft power. Suppose this person is going into a meeting with a room full of people in various chaotic moods. Going in as themselves only means they are subject to the whims and mood swings of whoever decides to be the loudest voice for leadership in that room. But there is another option. They could tune in to the energy of potential of the meeting, call it into the room, and fill the air with that potential. They are then the stewards of the energy in the room. They're holding the space for something wonderful to happen even if they never speak a word. It's energetic, working with the power of what wants to be.

7. In soft power, people become energetically aware and from this place begin to utilise their energy (passion, vision, potential, creation, etc.) to move things into play. They are accessing their power, but they are not necessarily recognised for it. They step out of the equation and let the energy act through them.

- **Coaching vibrant, creational power** – In soft power, there tends to be very little movement generated other than what is initiated as the potential is made available. But in vibrant, creational power, there's a lot of movement and dancing, there is the continual sparking off of next levels of play. So in vibrant, creational power, you as coach must guide the client to good creatorship where they accept a level of ownership and power for how things are turning out. In fact, it's very likely at this point, that you'll be immersing them into the energy of their own passions and visions and having leadership conversations with them how to fulfil them creatively.

1. Have your client connect to creation in whatever way is right for them in that moment. Be sure to point them towards vibrant creation in whatever way you can. It's the energy of pure creation, new creation, evolving creation, and so on. Ask them to immerse themselves in the sparkle of creation and possibility, "sparkle" being a key word to point them to the vibrant connection.

2. Now that they're connected to vibrant creation, ask them to describe how it feels. Do they come more alive? Are they feeling more energy move through them? Has the quality or frequency of the energy changed from their personal energy in soft power to creative energy in vibrant power? Ask them these questions and through conversation, get them conscious of the creational shift.

3. Ask them to connect with the potential of what wants to be through them now. Allow them to play and to discover their own unique relationship to creation and how it works through them and for them.

4. In soft power, the client is walking in the reality of what is, bringing something more to it. But in creational power, they actually walk as the power of creation. They carry their reality with them and bring that reality to the places they work, live and play. So in the example of holding the space for the meeting, they can use their vibrant, creational power to create the space from the potential and then activate that space as its own creation. They don't "hold" anything; it's not happening with their personal power. It's the power of the potential being created and they're the initiators or creators. It is still them and it, but it's so much more power that they had before.

- **Coaching alchemical power** – This is coaching the step from personal to ALL.

Have them expand their energy beyond the cosmos—all the while staying centred in themselves in the physical—in order to discover the sense of All-ness. This initial move tends to be a state of expansive, calm knowingness. You want to encourage them from there to step into the power of All, to own it and to be willing to source it into reality. The people who tend to make this move the most graciously are those who have already decided to give up who they think they are and what they've been up to, to discover an emerging sense of newness in themselves. So, as the coach, encourage your client to let go of their view of themselves and to be willing to become, become, become. This willingness ignites everything else into alchemical becoming. It is the magical ingredient.

Another option is to have them make the step from soul to Living Soul (the newly emerging Life source). Taking this step integrates this sense of All-ness into a living experience quite easily actually and there's less difficulty in making the move.

The final step occurs when they move essence to essentiALLity, evolving their raison d'etre or purpose.

But taking the step into Living Soul and All doesn't guarantee alchemical power. You can access it from there, but you don't necessarily become it. So what does it take to become it? Try this, first on yourself and then with clients who you know are willing:

1. Guide them to connect with and return to the origin of their source. Just have them try it and see what happens. Each person may take a different route or go to a different place. Just let their inherent knowing guide the journey for them.

2. Once there, have them find their current overriding purpose or raison d'etre and track it back to its source. Write it down for them. This is important. You'll see why in a minute.

3. Once they've found that overriding raison d'etre, have them become it completely. Let them revel in this for a few minutes or even for a few sessions if they really love that connection to their current source.

4. When the time is right, ask them to put that purpose or raison d'etre into al-

> chemical evolution and allow it to evolve. Let it and them find their way naturally to their next and new level of source. What generally happens here is that they discover a massive, alchemical context from which they live from that moment forward *and* that continually evolves itself. They may actually be surrendering their humanity as they knew it and moving into the evolution of the human race as something sparklingly brand new.

EXPERIENTIAL PRACTICE: GETTING IT OUT THERE

- What levels of power are you currently working at? Are you ready to move to the next levels? If not, what thoughts come up around your "no"? Take a look at those thoughts and see if they're real, and if not, move them on. Then ask the question again and see if you're committed to working to your next levels of power. You could just intend to move to your next level of power and see what happens. You could also try it on energetically and see how you like the feel of it. Play with it, adventure in it, and discover what you can about you and your next levels of power.

- Take a buddy in the course and work together to evolve your raison d'etre, if it's wanting to be evolved.

- Consider the possibility that all coaching orients around moving people into greater levels of leadership and power in their lives. So instead of taking on a specific client or two to move them forward, try orienting yourself as a coach coaching leadership and power in people, if that suits your work and raison d'etre. See how that alters your coaching. As a coach, track people's journey towards leadership and power and guiding them forward on that path to a life of fulfillment. Play with this in your coaching and in your life. Bring leadership and power graciously into all that you are and do. But don't just stop there. After all, you're now an evolutionist. What are you going to do to evolve leadership and power in the world today?

Close your eyes, become the power of All, and connect to all other beings who stand in alchemical power for our collective and conscious evolution and see how that feels. What's different? What do you discover there about intelligence, connectivity, thought, brain functioning, creation, and so on? Stand in something you don't yet know about and see what's evolving. But even as you acknowledge that you don't know anything about it, realise that you and we are its creators and on some level we have already created this possibility for evolution. And now we're living it into being. This leads us brilliantly into our third course in Advanced Coach Training: AlchemicAll Power.

BREAKTHROUGH

The thing with All-ness and with alchemical power is that it isn't just you doing it. Even though you can be it and do it as a single being, it is so interconnected that it's actually a collaboration of everything and everybody, of all Life everywhere. This is such a huge subject, such a massive possibility, that it literally holds the evolution of our race in its very being. The breakthrough of this chapter is a complete evolution of humanity, as well the introduction of a brand new level of leadership and power!

Perhaps the human race has moved on and perhaps a brand, new sentient source consciousness is already flooding our every cell. Our latest becoming is only the tip of a collective way of being together that presently we can only guess at. The more we live it, the more we dance together within it, the more it alchemically becomes, and the more the human race moves beyond humanity into something magnificently brand new.

THE LIVING SOUL COURSE WRAP-UP

Congratulations on completing the Living Mind and Living Soul courses!

You are now at the point of becoming an evolutionary agent and a source for evolutionary power and leadership in the world today. It is from here that we begin the journey into collaborative leadership and power, into our collective evolution. Moving forward, we invite you to participate as mindful co-creators of the next leaps we will generate individually and collaboratively. Get your evolutionary caps on!

COURSE THREE

EVOLU
TION

CHAPTER I
VISIONARY STEWARDSHIP

Intention Of This Chapter
- To create a powerful new way of bringing creative genius and vision fulfilment into the world.
- To dance in a bigger game with whole new levels of potential that are just waiting to be brought into reality.

Profound Potential
- To access what wants to happen through us, on the highest levels, in every moment.
- To achieve evolutionary results and have the most amazing time doing it!

Key Elements

1 — What is visionary stewardship?
Co-creating with the profoundly powerful energy of potential

2 — Leadership, power and vision fulfilment in the new paradigm
Surrendering to the magic of the energy

Exploratory Discussion
1. What is visionary stewardship?
2. How do you tune in to possibilities and potential while coaching?
3. How do you access and then coach vision?
4. How do you access and then coach ultra-creativity?
5. How do you become the creator of your reality?
6. How do you coach others to create reality of their choice?

ESSENTIAL CONTENT

1 — What is visionary stewardship?

Today we're living in a new millennium and a brand new paradigm of reality. This is an era of visionary stewardship, where we're taking ourselves into new levels of creative entrepreneurship, dynamic business, and sourceful reality creation.

Visionary stewardship is a step beyond self into partnering with and becoming creation itself.

It reaches beyond you and what you think you're capable of and what you think you want. It occurs when you dance in the moment with the energy(ies) of something magnificently brand new in order to empower and create it into being. While these energies will match your own passions and interests they far surpass anything you want or desire. When you partner with and become these new energy potentials, there is so much more on offer than you could ever imagine possible: abilities, synchronicities, synergy, collaboration, and so on.

Visionary stewardship comes from co-creating with the profoundly powerful energy of potential. In this move, you become more than you have ever imagined you could be. As a visionary steward you take on and walk as multiple energy potentials. You discover a brand new paradigm of play.

The visioning process in the old paradigm goes something like this:

You come up with an idea or vision based on a logical understanding of the market and what it wants. Traditionally, it has been a single idea or a static vision based on an extension of the past (e.g. market trends, projections, and so on). Generally, the visions are based on what you want or what you think others want

The attainment of the vision is goal oriented, with a project plan outlining how you're going to achieve the vision. You mobilise your resources and move step by step until you achieve what you set out to achieve. You know where you want to go and how you intend to get there. There are rarely any leaps in what is possible from this approach.

The vision is generally held by one person who directs, pushes, and pulls the process until the vision is achieved or fails. The responsibility of the vision being achieved falls on that one person. And even when they try to get others to buy into it, it is often difficult to translate the passion and energy of what they are trying to achieve to others.

Even in the most creative approaches, people come up with lots of ideas and then rationalise what will or will not work practically. By the time ideas are implemented they are hugely watered-down versions of what was originally an exciting idea full of great energy.

Leadership around visioning in the old paradigm is burdensome--you either have huge tasks you have to take on all by yourself or you have to work hard to engage others in what you want them to do. If you're the leader and the one holding the vision, then everyone has to keep coming back to you in order to move things forward.

In this old paradigm approach to visioning, goals and targets are set and then become rigid. Often the reasoning behind them is lost in the drive to achieve at all costs. In many cases, things do not go smoothly and there may be a good amount of struggle and stress. And sometimes even with all that, people just don't achieve their goals. Why is that? Because they're not working with what wants to happen. They're rigidly trying to achieve something in the old way, trying to push it into play with their own personal energy, and not using the powerful energetic resources of potential dancing into reality. They get stuck in the goals, unable to be fluid, creative, and inventive in the moment, so the goals actually become boxes that capture and limit their passion and creativity.

In the new paradigm, it's quite different—fluid, dynamic, in the moment, ultra-creative, and not based on what the market wants and will bear, but instead on what wants to come through now. You tap into the energy of the vision and become it so that everything you do is immersed in this passionate, creative energy. Consequently, visioning in the new paradigm has more momentum, more creativity, more passion, more drive, more spontaneity, and a lot more collaboration because people want to play with it.

Visionary stewardship in the new paradigm goes like this:

You are working powerfully with and for what wants to happen through you in the world now. This is the space where mega leaps occur.

Once you touch, bring through, and work with and as what wants to happen, you become the steward for a multiplicity of visions. Why is this? Because you're working with multiple potentials that want to come through you now and you're not attached to just one thing. You move into a bigger, greater view of everything and you see that as you move one potential into play, so the others move more fluidly as well. You become the greater, bigger dance of Life, of everything, and you discover that you're more committed to the dance than to any one specific thing.

Leadership in this paradigm is light, playful, and amazingly powerful. You collaborate with others in a leaderful way, with everyone in the energetic dance contributing what is theirs to give. Everyone is uniquely in their own leadership and everyone is excited to be a part of the vision coming alive and real in the world.

The visions you access are sparkling new, never before seen. They're not anchored in the past; they have been energetically co-created in the now for a glorious new future. The attainment of these fluid visions comes from a dance of energies, with resources appearing as and when they are needed.

You access super-creativity and know that anything is possible when you act as and for the energy. Implementation results in the creation of something spectacularly new. You are not caught in the trap of worrying how things will be received. You are working with what wants to happen in the world now and know that it will land in perfection.

What is sourcing the visions that you become the steward for? These new potentials come from a whole new source of creation, a place where brand new possibilities abound. They come from a wellspring of new creation, of Life bringing itself alive. It's as if brand new options for creative living and being are alway on offer to us. They live in the air all around us, just waiting to be breathed in, called to, and lived into being. There are so many new possibilities waiting to be brought into being, that every person on the planet could choose a million each and they'd still keep on coming. The air is explosive with potential.

If you try to look at potential from the existing status quo of humanity and the world as it's always been, then you can miss these new potentials. You have to be willing to look for them beyond everything that's known, but you don't have to go way out there to get them. You can stand for and be open to limitless thinking and creating right here, right now. That may sound a bit daunting and you might wonder if that's really possible. Yes it is. Simply stop thinking about how it's always been and be willing to call the next newest new that wants to be now. It's attracted to you and you are a magnet for it. This is the magic of the new paradigm. You play in the moment with a commitment to the highest potential in all that you do and it just pours in to play with you.

These new potentials are called to you as a result of your own passions and visions as well as your being on both the physical level and on a vaster level of yourself. They come in response to your own energetic commitment to a brand new future for us all. Even though the energy of these new potentials seems to come to you on one level, on another level you are consciously creating them and calling them to you. This occurs as the vastness of you works with the vastness of creation and possibility now. It is a huge collaborative creation! And it occurs in the greater, vaster energy fields that ripple consciousness into reality with great grace and ease.

Exercise

· **Becoming a visionary steward**

1. **Entering the world of possibilities and potential** – In order to enter the world of this conversation (it actually is a different world and reality) you must re-orient yourself from a world of problems, issues, challenges, and chaos to a world of possibility, potential, passion and play.

How do you do that? Well, simply say it is so and mean it! You can choose this reorientation at will in any moment. And you can choose it permanently if you so desire. It's not something that has to be worked towards. Go for it and see how it feels.

If you can't say yes to it immediately, see what thoughts come up for you as to why you don't want to. Put those thoughts in front of you in the light of day and see if they're really real right now. Would you choose these thoughts as your indicator of choice and fulfilment? If not, toss them in the bin. Throw them away. They're not doing you any good sitting in there inside of you holding you back from what you really want to do and are really here for. Keep doing that till the space is clear. Give the thoughts no energy whatsoever. Just keep tossing them in the bin till you're clear. Then choose to reorient.

Remember that you're an amazing being in an incredible time of constant and continuous evolution. Don't get hung up in the little things. Be big, be bold, be daring, be courageous, and inventive. Choosing to see potential and possibilities doesn't mean anything other than declaring that you're ready to play.

2. **Become the energy of the potential** — Whether you are working on the next steps of an existing project, or bringing through a completely new vision, the steps are the same:

- Take a deep breath and feel yourself expand from your centre until you are in your most magnificent, expanded state.
- Call to you the energy of the highest potential for what wants to happen through you now (you can make this specific to a project or leave it open).
- Bring that energy present in whatever way feels natural to you, and then breathe it up through you, and out through your high heart area. Keep repeating this alchemical breathing until the energy is all out in front of you.
- Then ask it what it is and ask any questions you would like to know about it, before making the decision as to whether you would like to partner it.
- If the answer is no, there's no problem. The energy and the potential will go to someone else who is ready to work with it now.
- If the answer is yes, then step into the energy and become it fully and powerfully. Own that this is who you are on your most magnificent levels.
- You can do this with many potentials and when you walk as the energy fields of multiple potentials, you become more than you ever imagined possible!

3. **Work as and from these new energies** — Visionary stewardship is about working as and from the energies, rather than working from one's personal energy with other energies. How are these different? The energy is co-created with you and what wants to happen. You're part of the whole big energy system. But if you work with the energy of you — which means, staying separate from the energy of the potential — then your conscious mind will get in the way rather than being part of the collaborative, co- creative dance. If you become the energy of the potential and work as the energy, then everything lines up with it and this is where new dynamism, super-creativity, synergy, and synchronicity pop into play to make it all happen. It takes the struggle out of the process and puts the lightness of touch into the whole dance.

4. **Start playing in the energy fields of the greater visions** — Are you willing to work for the greatest, magnificent expression of what wants to happen now, the highest potential for this world and beyond? If you are, you'll find yourself much more in touch with these new visions and possibilities. As you step into them, you become those energy fields walking in the real world.

You can actually walk as multiple energy fields, multiple visions, or possibilities expressing themselves. This new paradigm of play isn't singular or linear in any way, shape, or form. It paradoxically allows many things to happen simultaneously and they all bounce off one another or leverage one another to make each one more than it is. It's about bringing multiple potentials into play to create and invent something much more rich and new.

5. **Be willing to reinvent yourself completely in the moment** – Being a visionary steward means that you get to reinvent yourself completely, totally brand new in every moment. You can be anything you want to be from this moment on and in being willing to reinvent yourself, you can alter everything.

Once you're in this place, you'll begin to see that you are continually letting go of anything old and unworkable. You get really comfortable with letting go of projects, thoughts, beliefs, ways of being, personality characteristics, historical input and learned behaviour that no longer have any energy for you. This brings delightful momentum to the process and keeps the ball rolling. This is new dynamism.

It could be said that it's about living completely in the moment, but it's actually a bit more than that. It's about living in the moment *and* fulfilling a new future now. It's weaving your visions of the future into the now that gifts us its magic, its lightness, its play and its power.

6. **Become the creator of your reality** – In this space, you become the creator of the reality in which you live. You realise that the old rules are only boxes, just things that someone made up once. Why do we need to give them any energy now? There is no set way that things are that you have to live into.

Perhaps the world is as you see it to be. As you see it, so it is. From this orientation, you can create how you want the world to be, then walk in and as it. Your imagination is such an amazing tool and we're suggesting you move imagination from child-like play into a reality creation tool.

2 — Vision fulfilment in the new paradigm

In the new paradigm, you can't quite figure things out by logic or reason. You have to be willing to let the magic happen and allow for creative invention beyond what you can think it to be.

Leadership in the new paradigm means being willing to step boldly where no one has gone before and to lead others graciously and powerfully into the dance of creative, evolutionary becoming.

The power here is that of inventive, limitless creation alive in the world. It sparkles, it dances, it weaves, ducks, and dives ... and yet it has backbone, incredible strength and presence. There is nothing that this leadership and power cannot dance with. It embraces and alchemically loves into being all that is great, excellent, spectacular, and amazing for all.

Fulfilment of visions in the new paradigm begins with surrendering all that you know about how to make things real. You surrender to the magic of the energy and it's not a passive act. It's a co-creative, sourceful, mega act. You enter fully into the dance and surrender any thoughts of how you think it should go. From your partnership with, and surrender to the music and the dance, the most incredible, artistic, creative excellence is created. When you become the music and the dance, it takes you to an unknown level. Now let's bring this level of mega-creation to every aspect of living, working, playing and being... so that All Life becomes that dance.

There are many steps to making a vision real and we've listed many of them throughout this chapter. But like a dancer, if you stop to measure each step and to be certain you've got it right, then you miss the pure and utter magic of surrendering completely to the music and the dance. The great artists of our world have always known this state. Now it's time to apply it to the living of Life in all that we do. It's time to live vibrantly, elegantly, richly, wondrously, and magnificently as the visionary stewards that the whole of the human race can become.

As opposed to traditional visions, you're already impacting the world from minute one by bringing the new potential in. Whatever you're doing has a much bigger reach immediately and is impacting the world and beyond. The power originates in the being of who we really are, combined with the power of the potential itself. The two in a dance are extraordinary. Have fun playing with potential on all its levels and discovering yourself as a visionary steward for the new!

EXPERIENTIAL PRACTICE: GETTING IT OUT THERE

- Work with what wants to happen rather than what you want.

- Step into the energy of the greater / higher potential and become it.

- Don't set goals. Instead dance each moment in ultra-creativity, with what wants to happen combined with what you love to do.

- Call others into a collaborative dance around it. They will want to come play because the call is strong and fun. They are called to the energy of it and they begin co- creating along with you. You don't have to be the only one carrying the responsibility of the vision or project fulfilment.

- Stop, tune in, and see what the energy wants now whenever you feel stuck. Perhaps this is guidance to go in a different direction or take a different tact. Perhaps there is new potential waiting to be realised.

- Have fun. If you're taking it too seriously and not having a good time, you can actually destroy the energy. New potentials and enlivening visions are fun create and play with. Anything else isn't really new.

BREAKTHROUGH

The breakthrough of this chapter is a new paradigm in which every being is stepping beyond self to partner with and become creation itself. It is about sourceful reality creation for the evolution of a future that is beyond our wildest dreams and imaginings.

CHAPTER II
ALLCHEMY

Intention Of This Chapter
- To unfold the evolution of alchemy to ALLchemy and to illuminate it as a new Life science and profession
- To be able to use your magical abilities
- To really get what it means to work as All energy and consciousness for transformation, creation and evolution… or even just for fun!
- To be able to work within and for an ever new and evolving collective awareness

Profound Potential
- For every person in this course to master the evolutionary art of ALLchemy and in doing so, to burst a new way of working into the world
- The elevation of humanity to a completely new kind of being
- The evolution of beingness everywhere

Key Elements

1 — Alchemy and ALLchemy
What's the difference?

2 — Taking the step from alchemy to ALLchemy
Owning the power and the totality of working as and for All

3 — ALLchemical coaching
Discovering the source in you as the source of ALL

Exploratory Discussion
- How do you access and define your Alchemical power?
- How do you experience your Alchemical power?
- How can you use your magical coaching abilities?
- How can you coach collective intelligence?

ESSENTIAL CONTENT

1 — What is the difference between alchemy and ALLchemy?

The movement from alchemy to ALLchemy is an energetic step. It's the move from personal human beingness into a living ALL source presence of new being. It involves:

1 – Creating anew

Although alchemy is thought of as creating something out of nothing, it is actually about transmuting one thing to another. With ALLchemy we are working directly with creation and with the new. It really is coming from nothing and becoming something. We don't look at what is. We look beyond that to create on the level of pure potential and pure consciousness, and in that movement, we birth something tangible and new.

2 – Being the energy of All

The biggest difference between alchemy and ALLchemy is the energy fields that you work in, with, and as. If you try to access alchemy now you may notice a shrinking back into the personal energy field to make something happen, but with ALLchemy you work as All, for All and the personal reflection and orientation disappears.

With alchemy you're working with universal energy as you. In ALLchemy you become the field of All and everything where evolutionary possibilities abound. And it doesn't occur as work in any sense of the word. It's a completely different experience. It ecompassess your totality of being, not only what you're doing.

3 – The totality of Life, Creation, Evolution, and Source

Alchemical awareness contains (or contained) the wisdoms and knowledge of all the alchemists through time. But ALLchemical awareness is a sentiently present Life force that you step into. It's an amalgamation of all the awareness everywhere through time and beyond time. It's the living presence of a new sourceness. As this presence, what there is to be, create and do naturally occurs as a powerful, energetic movement with, as, and for ALL. This presence is the totality of Life enlivening itself more alive, creating more creation, evolving more evolution, and sourcing more sourceness.

2 — Taking the step from alchemy to ALLchemy

With ALLchemy, we are asking you to own the power and the totality of working as and for All, to let go of you as you've known you, and to move into an ever-evolving new beingness, willing to dance vibrantly and ALLchemically within it and as it.

As you take this step you become the full living totality and presence of that which you stand for and are working for and as. It's an ever-evolving, mega-beingness.

In connecting with and becoming All, you must be willing to "surrender" all other views of yourself. This is a mega-leap into the beyond. It feels like surrendering, but it's not really surrendering. It's not even death / rebirth. It's completely and totally letting go of the individual and personal and from this new space of totality, they are no longer even relevant. You stop putting your energy into things that concern you personally and at the same time, you're the ultimate source in the cosmoses, so you are also taking care of yourself. All parts of you fully align with ALL, everything, Life enlivening and evolving itself. From there flows a natural, organic, and continual movement into being new in every moment. You then move fully into the creational moment of being / becoming / creating creation / sourcing sourceness / evolving evolution. You become a full source of reALLity creation.

Once you've made the transition into the evolutionary paradigm, here are some of the characteristics that you will experience as ALLchemical living:

· **Extreme self-care** — In ALLchemy, there is a real compulsion about what you need to be doing in every moment. You are compelled to move with the energy of what wants to happen. It's an invitation, but an extremely compelling one. You realise you need to take care of yourself and have more fun. You have moved into crystal clarity and your energetic sensing dictates how you treat yourself. You know what to do in every moment and there is a lightness and joy about it. You are looking to be the best version of you / us / ALL / Life in every moment.

· **True abundance** — Every occasion is a special occasion, an opportunity to celebrate the magnificence of everything in Life. After all, if Life is enlivening itself as and through you, then how can your life be anything but joyful abundance!

· **Lightness of touch** — This new beingness is not so serious and significant. We can have huge fun while we are creating mega cosmoses! In the past people felt the need to "change the world." It felt serious, heavy, and burdensome because it was anchored in what we did not like about the world. Now we know that none of the past is real and is fast passing into oblivion. It doesn't serve to work in this serious, old, "change things'" kind of way. We are stepping into this vibrant, amazing ALLchemical game where everything is new. And what's really great about all this is that we have brought ourselves to this point. It's not about believing anything - it's about being and exploring. So have fun exploring. We have moved into a completely new space and new beingness, so play in it. What are the new rules? Are there any rules? Should there be any rules? Celebrate, enjoy and delight in this new experience—and stop making it so significantly serious! Have fun.

· **Collaborative working** — Collaboration itself is experiencing a mega shift. In our earlier collaborations, we would tune in to what wanted to happen and then we would pretty much all get the same answers and sensings. But there's a place in ALLchemy where one holds things in absolute perfection and it will go there because that person as ALL / everything / Life can see it that big. If any one of us holds the perfection of something as ALL, as Source, then it will turn out no matter what anyone else in the collaboration senses in the moment. In order for this to happen there must be support, knowing, trusting, and allowing from the rest of the collaboration, a total trusting that this one person has it in perfection for the most brilliant outcome.

· **No separation** – You are tuned in; you don't have to stop and tune in anymore. It's seamless. You are so "in the moment" that the need for planning and preparation begins to disappear. You don't have to go and get the energy of what wants to happen, because you are in it, of it and as it. In the past, we would tune into the energy of what wanted to happen through us, call this up and then co-create with it. It was us working with our own awareness. But now, in the ALLchemical dance, we are awareness walking and talking. We're not working with it, we are it. We are creating as it in every moment. There is no separation. This creates a gorgeous, exciting, fluid and continuous movement in a very mega and gracious way.

· **The availability of everything** – Everything is already there. You can call more of it up, but in essence everything is available to you in the moment. All possibilities are just waiting, expectantly, vibrantly, in the air around us. From here, everything comes alive.

· **A bigger, more beautiful mega-dance** – Everyone and everything is involved in the dance of Life in a way that they were not before. Life is sentient and alive and there's a much bigger, vibrant dance. You find yourself communicating with seemingly inanimate objects—a tree, a telephone line, a stone—and you know that you are communicating with Life. This is you in total collaboration, all the time, with everything. And more than that, you are its ALLchemist calling Life more alive through every single thing you do, see, breathe, speak, and touch.

ALLchemy is when you can hold something in its fullest perfection in its fullest capacity. You're not separate from it in that moment. You are it. As ALL, you move completely into the flow of energy, keeping in tune with what's wanted and needed in each moment, but also being the source of the ALLchemical movement at the same time. You alchemise yourself, it and ALL and grow stronger and stronger in the movement of it.

When we are fully in alignment with and know that we are everything / ALL/ Life / living consciousness walking, we are ALLchemical in everything we do. In the transformation process, it's like every cell in your physical being is realigning - there is a realignment of you / ALL on every level.

Exercise

· **Smoothing the transformation to ALLChemy** – As pioneers, the transformation can sometimes feel like a challenging process. But as more of us take this step, it becomes easier and easier... until suddenly everyone is there and there's nothing to it at all. Here are some ways to make the process a little easier.

- **Create an evolutionary ceremony** — Mark the end of the old and the beginning of the new. This could be writing a list of everything you are letting go of, and another of everything you are embracing. As soon as you have done this, you have moved into another energetic space, so you can tear up both lists, and let them go too.

- **Let go of the past. It is no longer real** — When things from your past or old ways of thinking pop up, there is huge power in realising that none of these are real. They're just an imprint from the past... a game that you've been playing, a false construct. The evolutionary paradigm is the reality now. So when anything of the past comes up, know it is not real. Honour it, love it, let it go, and revel in the ALLchemical moment. You choose where to put your energy and your creations.

- **Exchange experiences** — Be in the conversation. Continuously and collaboratively talk to others in the evolutionary paradigm about your experiences. It helps move the transition through and in your understanding some of the things that are happening to you. When you can see the bigger picture beyond just yourself, it reorients the whole experience into one of grace and ease.

3 — ALLchemical coaching

Working in ALLchemical consciousness is taking us into a new level of coaching, evolving the field into something brand new. We're working now in an increasingly new, collaborative awareness. Well beyond collaborating to achieve an individual's personal goals and visions, we are working in new ways that in a wisp of a moment can sparkle up a new beingness beyond anything seen before. We are doing things in every moment that will stun and amaze you as a coach, let alone your clients.

As ALLchemical coaches, you're invited to recreate a brand new relationship to Life in every moment, to become the movement of Life towards the new. You move into movement with the magic and start dancing with what wants to happen for your clients, with you as the source of that movement. You become the magicALL fields. You are ALLchemy. You are everything and ALL but until you own it, it's elusively something separate from you.

To become a cosmic ALLchemist you have to own it. Don't just surrender into it and dance with the energy. Become it. Be the magic. Be the new source sourcing itself.

As an ALLchemical coach, there is no separation between you and your client, yet of course there is because we are each uniquely everything. It's a beautiful paradox. If you're everything, then as an ALLchemical Coach, you can go inside yourself to find where the client truly lives as ALL they are and can be. Then the moment you touch that in you, they become themselves fully. It is not about going into them and becoming one with them. That tends to distort and disrupt the energetics. Rather, it's about you as ALL / everything / Life touching the place in you that is them.

On this level of becoming, they instantly integrate their greater self and touch their vaster self as well. But there's something more and new here as well. It's a new magicALL beingness that's brought into living reality. You fall madly, wildly, wondrously in love with them and they move graciously into the becoming. In this new becoming, they move gracefully beyond personal and individual and discover a natural and automatic move into a new, collaborative, conscious beingness.

This is about a completely new connection in consciousness. It's a different movement ... super, hyper grace with power and speed from deep, deep, eternally within and without at the same time. And it's this different movement that creates the new magicALLity. This new, collaborative, living totality of consciousness is inviting us ALL to coach the recreation of relationship with Life and with ALL always.

The key to how you get there with someone is you become mega ALLchemical living consciousness yourself. It's that ultra-connected magicALL flow state. It's not only about words. In this space, you fully and truly activate mega energetics or mega energy into the motion. It's stepping into the full expression of the mega -energy ALLchemically. You walk fully as that. You breathe fully as that. You can actually be silent and do THE most profound work.

You're working with ALL of you, with ALL of them and with ALL of the living consciousness / presence around you and within you both. You're working with being in totality. You've moved beyond working as an individual with another individual, to working as ALL with ALL, no matter who's sitting in front of you. And that's a joyful experience. It's not overwhelming necessarily. It's simply about owning the ALLchemy and being the source of it in everything you do.

Do you see the movement we've made from day 1, course 1— from mind and individual self to to mega beingness ever-evolving itself?

We've also moved from personal potential to profound (world-changing) potential, to pure (evolutionary) potential and then to mega potential. Mega potential also involves evolution, but in a different kind of way. There's more power in it and it's a more solid experience. You grow fully into yourself and there's more substance to it and you. There's a maturity and a coming together of what wants to happen into a much greater sense of sustainable movement and living presence. In the world now, many people have stepped from individual being to mega being and by doing so, we've created a groundswell of possibility and of "reALLity" that did not exist before this time. Because so many people have stepped fully into and owned this cosmicious mega creation, a whole new reality is now alive and dancing! It's unprecedented and each of you has been a key player in and source creator of this mega creation.

Exercise

· **Coaching your clients' magicALL becoming** – There are likely a multiplicity of ways to do this. Here's one gracioUS and naturALL way to this becoming:

Picture your client in front of and outside of you. Now as the ALL that you are, as living consciousness walking, as the source of new, as the everything and ALL, find the place in you that is so expansively in love with them that you can hardly believe it.

Dive deeply within to the eternal new you/them and ALLchemically mega love them into being / becoming. As you experience that moment of ecstatic bliss within yourself that comes knowing / seeing / honouring / loving them, they will graciously, zestfully, and wondrously move into their becoming. You've just unlocked a magicALL door for them. Look inside yourself for your connection to them, for your mega relationship to them, for your awe for them open the door. This isn't about finding the client's "issues" in you and dealing with them there, nor is it about becoming one with them. It's about discovering the source in you as the source of ALL and then falling madly, passionately, profoundly in love with ALL that they are as the evolution of being. Then magicALLy they are its becoming.

As coach you are fully the source of ALL. From this space you do not hesitate. You lose any kind of filter for what wants to be said or done. You go for it instantly and wondrously. It's a magicALL moment both for you and for them. And it ripples through ALL consciousness to touch ALL of Life everywhere. These are truly ALLchemical, magicALL moments that stir the passions of Life. This kind of mega-grace applies with everything in ALLchemical working. You don't have to try very hard. It's magicALL. It happens in a breath, in a thought, in a whoosh without really thinking about it. And yet you are super conscious about it for sure.

EXPERIENTIAL PRACTICE: GETTING IT OUT THERE

- Have fun exploring as All. Don't just surrender into it and dance with the energy. Become it. Be the magic. Be the new source sourcing itself.

- Find the place in you that is so expansively in love with Life and connect to it to become Life, evolve Life, and alchemically create new Life.

BREAKTHROUGH

The breakthrough of this chapter is mega-evolution in the evolutionary paradigm. As the collective, collaborative consciousness we have shifted from creating, initiating, driving and getting people to the evolutionary paradigm to living inside of it. More than just doing a coaching course on moving people into greater passion and vision, we've co-created a reality that's never been before. Now that's mega evolution!

CHAPTER III
CREATIONAL LIFE POWER

Intention Of This Chapter
- To evoke the ultimate liberation of your creational Life power
- To ALLchemically activate creational Life power in those you coach

Profound Potential
- To move beyond knowing to creational understanding and the instantaneous reality creation it offers

Key Elements
1 — Creational Life power
The source of new energies and abilities

Exploratory Discussion
- How do you access and define your creational power?
- How can you evoke creational life power in your and others?
- How do you coach creational life power?

ESSENTIAL CONTENT

1. Creational Life power

In recent years a new Life source energy has emerged. It has flooded our cells and poured through the air around us. It has taken activation in physical form. People are beginning to work with and live with this new energy source that thrives and pulses all around and within us.

Creational Life power is the relationship that develops between you, your physicality, and the living creational presence that you are becoming. Creational Life power surges, pulses, and soars through form, filling it with a new surety and clarity. It's beyond any power that we've previously looked at in this programme. It's irreverent. It makes you laugh heartily with the sheer possibility of the moment. It's zestful, zinging, passionate, and ultra-creative. It's literally alive with potential and possibilities exploding everywhere. Limitless energy, unending possibilities.

In course one, The Living Mind, we looked at the move through mind, heart, spirit and soul into a vibrant sense of wholeness and aliveness. Then in course two, we moved beyond this personal wholeness to a collaborative, collective evolutionary becoming... the emergence of the evolutionary paradigm. In course three, we're exploring mega in great depth, only to discover in the writing of this, that we have once again evolved beyond mega and perhaps even beyond the evolutionary paradigm.

How can this be? Can evolution be moving this fast? Yes, it can and is. As we learn to be responsible and profoundly powerful Evolutionary Wayshowers, we are speeding up evolution and all that is associated with it (time, form, space, distance, language, intelligence, and more). While this may sound a bit unbelievable for anyone who hasn't experienced the previous levels of wholeness and vibrant reality in the evolutionary paradigm, it is readily accessible and understandable in the experience of those who are willing to surrender all that they have learned so far—not just in this course but in the whole of Life.

Creational Life power is most accessible in this clear space of no thought, no beliefs and no particular perception. It's an energy that infuses the spaces within you and all around you with a living presence of creation and more.

This doesn't mean you have to try to think about nothing. It's more like the willingness to dance openly in every moment for possibilities that defy possibility. It isn't reaching for what can be. It's the spontaneous and instantaneous reaction *and* creation that happens when the new Life power meets the wondrously open, dancing, living intelligence.

Creational Life power is leading us to many new things including:

· Neurogenesis – the ability to use the new Life source power to rejuvenate, revitalise and even completely redesign our physical and energetic structure and reality.

· Limitless thinking with limitless possibilities – seeing beyond everything that is or ever has been, and even past everything future that would have been. This thinking occurs independent of time, space and form and allows us to see vaster, greater, deeper and more creatively than we have ever done before.

- Inventive genius – no longer do you have to be born with a special gift. Anyone can access the musicality and wonder of creative genius and do with it what they will in the search for excellence and play!

We are moving beyond in so many ways: beyond healing, beyond spirituality, beyond human being, beyond traditional intelligence, and so on and so on. It is for these kinds of evolutionary creations that we have gifted ourselves with these new energies, powers, and abilities. Now it's our job to learn to do this well, striving ever for greater and greater understanding, connectedness and profound commitment to a Life that is ever-enlivening itself for ALL.

Exercise

- **Evoking Creational Life power in yourself and others** – It is an ALLchemical act. You reach both out and in to meet the living presence of new creation source and let the energy surge through you. You feel and experience the new Life source power, then you become the full presence of it ALL. To activate it fully in yourself simply "ping" it into being. It doesn't take much more than that actually. An ALLchemical act from the new beingness utilising the new Life source power is a millisecond experience. It's not even a breath. It's a mega-ping with a smile on your face and the sheer mega delight of watching this Life source power be activated in every cell and space within and around you. Life literally lights up around you. Your face will illuminate. Your eyes will sparkle. Your laughter will deepen. You are alive in a way you've never been before. And you know that you know the depths of the power you're living and it's more than you can know.

To activate this creational Life power for others, become it fully yourself. Revel in the clear, dancing moment. Feel it pulse and surge within you. Then reach out to where they stand and be with them—not in them, of them, or as them. Simply be with them. Invite them telepathically to join you in this ALLchemically dancing space. It's more like pulsing a wave form through the living fields, than it is actually sending a verbal telepathic message. Again, this all happens in an enriched millisecond, as if it's way beyond time. You are in the space of the totality of full rich being meeting and activating the totality of full rich being.

Do people have to be ready in some way for this? Probably, but not necessarily. It seems to happen naturally and of its own accord when it's right. It's not necessarily something you think of doing and then do. It's more like an opportunity that pops up in the moment to be delighted in.

It takes literally no energy from you at all. Far from it, it surges new energy through you, leaving you feeling marvellous and alive. It also leaves the other person feeling similarly. They smile. They stand straighter and truer. They laugh easier. They find a new strength in themselves and make a paradigm shift in that moment to the evolutionary paradigm or beyond.

> People whose creational Life power is activated find that they feel different. Sometimes it's subtle and sometimes it's mega. Don't create any expectations of what it should look or feel like. It's simply an activation of something that will last with them a very long time and even possibly for the rest of their lives, evolving always.

EXPERIENTIAL PRACTICE: GETTING IT OUT THERE

· To activate this creational Life power for others and become it fully yourself, connect to your breath. Be fully present. Then connect to new creation source and let the energy surge through you.

· To start coaching creational life power connect with clients telepathically. Allow this new energy to flow through you, leaving you and your client feeling vibrant and alive.

BREAKTHROUGH

The breakthrough of this chapter is possibly the very greatest gift that we have co-created in the last thousands of years. Yes, we have co-created Creational Life Power. We have pulled free, vibrant, alchemical, dynamic energy out of the spaces between the spaces, perhaps literally out of the great creative void and brought it present in the here and now for ALL of Life to be alchemically enlivened. The breakthrough of this chapter is joyful, limitless energy, and unending possibilities.

COURSE WRAP-UP: EVOLUTIONARY STRATEGY

A strategist is generally thought of as someone who sees the bigger picture and knows how best to move things from where they are now to the bigger potential they envision. They are visionaries who see beyond the present moment and beyond how things already are.

They see:

- multiple possibilities,
- the routes to them,
- the consequences and benefits of each,
- the one or ones that provide the optimum outcome and
- the most powerful ways to realize them now.

In business today, most strategic planners work from the past, adding generative models to create a slightly better version of what's already been and then look from the present, step by step forward how to make that happen. These strategists tend to see only what has been, what is, and where to linearly go from here to achieve a predictable outcome.

An Evolutionary Wayshower works from a completely different orientation. They look beyond what's ever been—way beyond the present to an unimaginable future that empowers everything we seek to achieve and dream. Then they stand in that unencumbered future and determine the optimal steps to bring it to reality.

But they're not just observers of the process. They're generative creators and visionaries who seek ultra-creative, inventive solutions in the now that produce transformative, miraculous, and unpredictable futures beyond anything that has ever been before. They are visionaries extraordinaire. They breathe, live, and create beyond all known boundaries and think beyond the current frameworks of thinking. They operate beyond the mind and beyond the boundaries of human thinking. They work in and for the new and dance outside of time constraints, physical constraints or any other kind of restraints to bring our most amazing dreams, visions and possibilities real. They are Evolutionary Wayshowers.

Evolutionary Wayshowers are a key, essential role in the evolution of humanity, of Life, and of All. They are not just working on projects, companies, education, politics, or for that matter any one single thing in this world. They're working on the whole of it: the future of human kind, of the Earth, of this evolving cosmos and beyond! They look not just to the impact we have on ourselves and our world. They look to the impact we have on everything everywhere.

An Evolutionary Wayshower is a master planner / architect / designer / creator / builder and implementer of our vast, co-creational future and how that future touches everything everywhere. While a visionary steward might take on a huge project or vision, an Evolutionary Wayshower would be the generator of the hugest, biggest picture of the whole totality of movement for ALL / everything now and in the future that that movement creates.

An Evolutionary Wayshower sees really big...

- beyond the current views and frameworks of thinking and
- beyond time to understand the wisdoms and learnings of the past as well as to look forward to the consequences and possibilities for new futures.

An Evolutionary Wayshower holds the responsibility and accountability for inventing Life strategies that allow for the greatest, vastest beingness, consciousness and realities to unfold.

Evolutionary Wayshowers not only dance in and impact awareness; they create and evolve it as well. They know that evolution is not a million-year process where we go merrily along for the ride. They know that every breath and every action we take has the opportunity, the potential, to evolve Life everywhere, on this Earth and beyond!

Evolutionary Wayshowers are ALLchemists, people who dance lightly in the time strands and consciousness webs of All and everything to alter that which has gone before and to create all that is possible in front of us. They are "NOW-ists," dancing beyond time to create all that they can envision now.

This is a role that one takes on proudly, profoundly, passionately and powerfully. No one should step lightly or unaware into this profession. It calls to those who are truly meant to dance within it, who are skilled beyond measure in creating cosmoses and in seeing beyond where they presently reside. Can a human body be the centre point for this much wisdom, knowledge and consciousness? Absolutely! It's what we were always designed to be and do. Perhaps that's exactly why we were created.

BECOMING EVOLUTIONARY WAYSHOWERS

The pre-requisites for the position or role of Evolutionary Wayshower are having learned about, experienced and mastered to at least some degree:

- the total alignment within yourself to working for the greater good of All and the trust that this engenders in you for all that you do
- a super-connection to Life and a total inability to do anything that would damage Life in any way
- the ability to see, sense and smell potential everywhere
- the masterful and spontaneous use of our ever-evolving evolutionary skills (knowing, innate sensing, telepathy, hyper-speed thinking, super-creativity and more) to ascertain what's the optimum movement to achieve potential in the moment and beyond
- the ability to explore all the various places beyond time, space and form, garnering wisdom and knowledge for the purpose of creating fresh wisdoms and knowledge in this moment now
- an expansive sense of new beingness, having moved beyond human being as we've always known it, to something much greater and vaster
- an ability to operate collaboratively in profound new ways
- an ease and grace of working energetically in the 'greater fields'
- a willingness to surrender everything that we know and are, taking it always to the next playgrounds of being, becoming, and beyond
- standing as a leader in the field of evolution in at least one specific area with a really good grasp of reality creation skills
- alchemy (the ability to work with higher, vibrant energies to spontaneously transform, create and evolve yourself, others and the world) and ALLchemy (the ability to supersede ALL that has ever been in any past, present or future to create in the moment the newest new from and for ALL)

We smile when we read the list, as many people on Earth think that it's crazy, that no one could be expected to fulfil this list, not in a single lifetime. But you and we know differently, don't we? We know that it is natural and completely doable—we have been opening ourselves to that reality since the beginning of this course.

All of these skills and abilities are required to some degree before you become an Evolutionary Wayshower. You don't want to be in the middle of evolving a different future, only to discover that your knowing isn't fully intact. And you certainly don't want someone else, without these skills, to be inventing that future for you and for us all.

EVOLUTIONARY WAYSHOWER CHECKLIST

- Are you aligned to work for the greater good of ALL?
- Do you trust yourself to always do that, no matter what?
- Are you aware of and in relationship with Life around you?
- Are you attuned to potential?
- Can you operate super-connected to Life? How often are you doing that now?
- Are you versatile with using knowing, innate sensing, telepathy, hyper-speed thinking, and super-creativity?
- Do you enjoy exploring, understanding, and creating new awareness?
- Do you create fresh new wisdoms and knowledge in the moment from a foundational understanding of (but not limited by) what has gone before?
- Do you experience yourself as a vast new being?
- Do you enjoy collaborating with others in the new?
- Have you learned how to work beyond your personal energy fields, dancing in the "greater fields"?
- Do you willingly surrender, on a regular basis, all that you know and are in order to discover the latest evolutionary new?
- Are you already a leader of an evolutionary vision or project?
- Are you able to work alchemically to transform, create, and evolve yourself, others, and our world?
- Do you believe that we have the ability to supersede ALL that has ever been in any past, present or future to create in the moment the newest new from and for ALL? If yes, have you had an experience of this yet?
- Do you have a passionate, burning desire to go bigger, to see further and to be a co-creator of a much, much bigger game?

Assume for the moment that you're the one who gets to decide whether or not you get hired for the position of Evolutionary Wayshower, even if it's an "in-training" position. Would you hire you based on your answers to these questions? Don't answer this lightly. Remember, this is our vastly wonderful, collective future we're talking about here.

Suppose that you're the one putting together a new council of Evolutionary Wayshowers to create and invent something entirely brand spanking, revolutionarily new. Would you accept you to be trained for the position? Can you see how even having to answer this question requires you to look at yourself from a completely non- personal perspective?

Breathe, relax, expand and super-connect. Tune in to your knowing and to the knowing in the living fields. Be certain that this is the right role for you to play. There may be other amazing and unique contributions for you to make besides this one, so be sure it's right for you and that you're right for it. Reach out to see if you feel that amazing call to take it always to the next and the newest levels.

If your answer is no, that's a-ok. Not everyone is meant to be an Evolutionary Wayshower... but wouldn't it be awesome if they were?

If you feel uncertain at this moment in time, then go back over the checklist to see where you're not playing on these levels and make a commitment to develop them. Many of the chapters of the Advanced Coach Training courses are designed to train people to become leading experts in these areas.

BREAKTHROUGH (AND BEYOND)

The breakthrough of this entire programme is to become Evolutionary Wayshowers who breathe, live, and create beyond all known boundaries, who think beyond the current frameworks of thinking, and who move forward the complete redesign of beingness-human and beyond.

Printed in Great Britain
by Amazon